The GoldenYearsTravel.com
GUIDE TO HOME EXCHANGE

Discover How to Swap Your Home
For Free Accommodations
Around the World

Sam and Judy Robbins

FIELDMOUSE PRESS
Washington, DC

Sam & Judy Robbins

FIELDMOUSE PRESS
Washington, DC

www.fieldmousepress.com

ISBN: 978-0-9911138-0-4

Disclaimer:

The authors and publisher make no representation or warranties with respect to the accuracy, applicability, fitness or completeness of the contents of this book. Therefore, if you wish to apply ideas contained in this book, you are taking full responsibility for your actions.

This book is dedicated to the community of home exchangers throughout the world who have pioneered and participated in this amazing way of experiencing our world through sharing homes, experiences and friendships.

Sam & Judy Robbins

Preface

When you and your family are away from your home, be it for a few days, a week, or a month or more, you're leaving unused a precious asset that could be used by another family hoping to visit, explore, and enjoy your part of the world.

If you will allow this asset to be used while you're away, there are other families who will do the same for you.

There's a community of many thousands of people out there—singles, couples, families, and retirees—that you can meet and join on the web sites of home exchange organizations. This book tells you how to do that and enjoy free accommodations, and often even a car to use, in countries around the world.

You may be surprised, as we were, to find yourself staying in some very elegant, luxurious exchange homes with pools, gourmet kitchens and wonderful outdoor spaces.

You may also be surprised, as we were, to find that there are many benefits and rewards to home exchange beyond the economic benefits. With the guidance of your home exchange partners, and often their friends and neighbors, you can experience the attractions and aspects of places you visit that you'd never have found on your own. You'll see how people live in other parts of the world, and perhaps bring back good ideas to use in your own home. To us—most rewarding of all—as you enjoy more and more home exchange experiences, you'll enjoy more and more lasting friendships around the world.

To date, we have enjoyed more than 70 home exchange experiences. Our purpose in writing this book is not only to introduce you to home exchange and encourage you to try it, but also to explain how you, too, can do it successfully.

Sam & Judy Robbins

Contents

Sam & Judy Robbins

Italy is a dream that keeps returning for the rest of your life.
—Anna Akhmatova

Introduction

Here's another reason to thank a teacher: It was teachers and other academics who pioneered the idea of exchanging homes in an organized way in the 1950s. Because they had summers off, they had plenty of time to travel but typically needed to do it less expensively.

Because home exchange offers so many compelling benefits —free accommodations with all the comforts of home instead of a cramped hotel room, sometimes a car or second home to use, the experience of living like a local, and opportunities to explore new places and make new friends around the world—over the years this movement attracted many other people. Like the home exchange pioneers, some needed to stretch their dollars, but all of them wanted to stretch their minds and truly expand their horizons.

In the early pre-Internet days, finding a suitable home exchange required a huge investment of time and trust. The few home exchange organizations then in existence typically issued annual catalogs, sometimes with quarterly or semiannual supplements containing new listings. The listing information, such as it was, consisted of a single postage-stamp size black and white photo of the house exterior or apartment interior accompanied by difficult-to-decipher coded entry items that attempted to describe some features of the home and the area.

When you spotted listings you thought might be suitable, you would write letters, send them off with a hope and a prayer that they'd be received and could be understood or properly translated

—and then wait. If you received a positive reply with a wonderful adventure ahead of you, your hard efforts all felt worthwhile. If you didn't, well, there was always next year.

Today, thankfully, home exchange organizations operate on the Internet. Click on a listing and you can usually see dozens of clear color photos, read lengthy descriptions of an exchange home's amenities and the attractions in its locale, correspond with your potential exchange partners in your language, knowing that if need be, your message can be translated into theirs, and when mutual interest exists, easily do as much going back and forth as needed to answer questions and make arrangements. It is no wonder then that today there are dozens of home exchange organizations, many thousands of families enjoying the benefits of home exchange, and many more hoping to do so.

As for us, we began exchanging homes back in the old printed catalog, postage-stamp photo days. As we retired or our work became portable, as our nest emptied, and as the Internet became widely available and used, we were able to become more involved and arrange many more home exchanges. All told, over the past decade, we've participated in more than 70 home exchanges in dozens of different countries—visiting places we had always dreamed of seeing, and seeing others we never dreamed existed. So you probably will not be surprised to know that we are always eager for opportunities to talk about home exchange and answer questions.

Invariably, people unfamiliar with home exchange ask, "But what about your stuff?" It's a question that over time we have come to understand has little to do with upstanding middle class families absconding with each other's toasters and televisions—and everything to do with trust and privacy.

Though in any aspect of life, it's wise to understand and protect against risks, happily, the overwhelming reports of home exchangers over the years have been extremely positive. The home exchange community has proven itself to be one of people who are both trusting and trustworthy. From the outset, each of you knows that while the care and protection of your home will be entrusted to others, so too, will theirs. This ethic of trust and shared responsibility helps explain why the most common attitude of home exchangers is that they want to leave the exchange home in as good or even better shape than they found it.

Of course, some everyday things can inevitably go wrong in the course of an exchange. You or your exchange partners could break a glass, forget to water a plant, maybe even dent a car. But really, most of these are not much different than the things that go wrong in everyday life. All of them can be managed effectively as long as you are reasonably adaptable and establish mutual understandings as you and your prospective exchange partners get to know each other.

Time and again, we meet veteran home exchangers who at first had reservations about entrusting their home to others, but soon discovered the greater peace of mind that comes with knowing there is someone to monitor the sprinkler system, care for their much-loved pet, or if need be, call the plumber before a leaky toilet becomes an expensive water bill. They now relish the pleasure of leaving home on yet another adventure knowing all will be well—and that, in the spirit of home exchange—on returning home they will probably find a lovely note and perhaps even a small thank-you gift where, some time before, they had left a welcome note and bottle of wine.

In over two decades of doing home exchanges, we have found our experiences to be rewarding in ways too numerous to count. At heart, home exchange is a gift of time. By dramatically shrinking our travel expenses, it offers us, God willing, many more weeks, months, even years, to greatly expand our travel horizons and experiences. Thanks to home exchange, we have been able to explore the rocky coasts of Maine and the Canadian Maritimes, live and shop like locals in Venice and Paris, snorkel off the beaches of Hawaii, Tahiti, and Australia, and so much more. Our exchange partners have generously shared not only their city town homes, beach villas, and country cabins, but also the ideas and insights that help visitors understand and appreciate each country's unique personality and sensibility. At the same time, their friends and neighbors, by welcoming us into their homes and lives, have reminded us ever so gently that even for prideful Americans, there are valuable lessons to be learned in every country and culture. It is our utmost hope that home exchanging brings you an abundance of all these same benefits and blessings.

On Giudecca, a Venetian artist paints on the sidewalk alongside the waterway across from St Mark's square.

What Exactly are Home Exchanges and Who Does Them?

A home exchange is an agreement between two parties—a single person, couple, family, or group of friends—to live in each other's homes for a period of time decided and arranged by the two parties themselves. The period of time can be a weekend, a number of weeks, even a month or more.

The home exchange can be for a vacation, visiting relatives when you don't want to impose, for weekend getaways, reunions, weddings, to learn a language, to visit where your ancestors came from, and the list goes on. You may want to do an exchange to be able to get introductions to local activities from exchange partners who live there, or to live like a local, not in a hotel.

In terms of arrangements, not all home exchanges are the same, and they tend to be offered and negotiated as "simultaneous" or "non-simultaneous." You may run into other terms—synchronous/non-synchronous, for example—but for our purposes here, we will use the more common terms: simultaneous and non-simultaneous.

Most home exchanges are simultaneous exchanges. These are essentially complete transactions in which each party stays in the home of the other at the same time. The great advantage of this arrangement is that each party fulfills its obligation to the other party while they are away from their home.

But some home exchanges are non-simultaneous in that each party stays in the home of the other at a different time. This works particularly well for people who have a second home they can retire to while exchange partners are in their primary home, but can also work if you don't have a second home but will be away on a cruise or other travel. Your exchange partners stay in your home while you are away, and you receive credit for a future stay in their home at a mutually agreeable time.

Still another kind of home exchange is a hospitality exchange, in which one party stays in its home while playing host to another and, at a mutually agreeable time in the future, the first-to-host party becomes the guest. An offspring of this type of exchange is a youth exchange in which two families, perhaps having met through a prior home exchange, arrange to each host one of the other's youngsters for a school year in another country, in part to achieve fluency in a new language.

Wherever you hope to travel, whatever kind of home exchange you seek, odds are you'll find a match. Until recent years, most home exchange activity took place in the US, Canada, Great Britain, France, Italy, Spain, in other smaller Western European countries, and in Australia and New Zealand. But today, home exchange activity appears to have reached a tipping point, with potential home exchange partners in every state in the United States and in over 150 other countries.

A cursory perusal of the major home exchange websites suggests that there are perhaps 200,000 singles, couples, or families who have listed their homes for exchange. We say perhaps because some members belong to more than one home exchange organization. If you were to browse through the listings of exchange homes, several things would stand out:

1. There is a great variety of homes ranging from simple to opulent, but typically each will be a comfortable home with comfortable beds, manageable kitchens, space to spread out and relax, and amenities such as TVs in one or more rooms, computers, wireless networks, bicycles, BBQ equipment and a porch, patio or deck to enjoy the outdoors. In some cases, there may be a pool, dock, and even the use of a boat. All this suggests that most home exchangers would describe their lifestyle as

comfortably middle class. This suggestion gains strength when you note that occupation-wise, the home exchange community includes many teachers, engineers, lawyers, doctors, nurses and other medical professionals, business owners and managers, and corporate and non-profit executives.

2. The vast majority of the homes are in countries where home exchange has been around the longest, but it is also noticeable that home exchange has gone global. One home exchange organization has 182 listings in China, 141 in Indonesia, 106 in Thailand, 57 in Singapore, 23 in Vietnam, 30 in the United Arab Emirates, 15 in Japan and 14 in Malaysia. Quite often, these are the homes of people who come from or who have lived in countries where home exchange is more common.

3. In organizations that identify experienced home exchangers, it's worth noting that a significant number of members have not yet participated in a home exchange. Perhaps that is simply because they have only recently joined and have not yet arranged an exchange; perhaps, though interested, they are waiting until the nest is empty and/or they are able to retire; maybe they are sitting back and waiting for someone to contact them; or it could be that their efforts to line up an exchange just aren't working because as newcomers to home exchange, they have not yet learned how to go about it in the best way.

Truth be told, when you're new to home exchange, it can be difficult to figure out how best to approach potential exchange partners. Understandably, you haven't yet gained a feel for how the process works, or how to best present your offer and communicate effectively with prospective exchangers. Though it may be unfair, experienced home exchangers are sometimes reluctant to contact newcomers because they feel, rightly or wrongly, that difficulties and misunderstandings are more apt to arise.

If you're a newcomer to home exchange or like the idea of becoming one, this book can help you overcome these potential problems and find your own place in the wonderfully enriching world of home exchange.

"Venice is like eating an entire box of chocolate liqueurs in one go."
— *Truman Capote*

How Does Home Exchanging Work?

Here in eight basic but essential steps, is how home exchange works. Each one is discussed in greater detail in a subsequent chapter.

1. First, you subscribe to one or more home exchange organizations. At the moment there are over 60 organizations which offer homes for exchange. They differ in many ways, including number of members, search capabilities, and features such as support for messaging. The next chapter is devoted to consideration of these organizations and how to decide which one(s) to join.

2. Then, you prepare your listing. While this may differ in some details depending on the organization where you are posting your listing, they all have fundamental similarities. A separate chapter of this book deals with your listing and provides advice on how to best represent your offer.

3. Next, you search for desirable exchange prospects in your places of interest and develop a list of favorites. This may sound simple, but it gets complicated. The reason being that while you work to identify your top choices in prospective homes, you also need to realistically assess the interest of the home's owner in exchanging with you. In the chapter How to Find Home Exchange Partners, you'll find the admittedly very subjective process we use to successfully line up exchanges in the places we

hope to visit.

4. Next, you rough out your itinerary and communicate with prospective exchange partners. This step requires you to be reasonable and flexible, but also to know the limits of your flexibility. For example, you may hope to visit Australia on a series of home exchanges that takes you to different areas in a certain order and during specific months. But, you also must be home in time for your favorite niece's wedding. Though you can't change the wedding date, you probably can work around it or visit Sydney before Adelaide instead of after.

5. Then, once you you know your approximate dates and destination, you can plan your trip. In consultation with your exchange partner, you can begin to research your travel options in earnest and establish specific dates and other details. Whether you both prefer doing so in a series of friendly emails, with or without a more formal, signed agreement, the goal is to come to a mutual understanding of all terms of the exchange.

6. Before you even begin to think about packing, you need to prepare your home for the exchange. When your exchange partners walk through your front door, you want them to feel welcome and comfortable in their surroundings. The chapter, *How to Get Your Home Ready for an Exchange*, is devoted to this process, and happily its effects often carry over and add to your comfort when you return home.

7. At last, you finally travel to your exchange home, and chances are you will find that your exchange partners have also endeavored to welcome you warmly and ensure your comfort in their home. Chances are, they already feel like friends.

8. After you return home, you communicate again with your

exchange partner, thanking them for the good care they took of your home. In many cases, you will have developed the sort of relationship that turns into a lasting friendship.

This seems a good point to mention in passing a phenomenon we have experienced in our years as home exchangers and that others have mentioned to us as well.

Essentially, what begins as a non-simultaneous exchange is not completed. One party to the exchange completes its visit, but the party that is owed an exchange never makes its visit.

Sometimes the reason for the exchange no longer exists. This happened in our case when we arranged a non-simultaneous exchange in a city where one of our sons and his family lived at the time. Our exchange partners came to our home for their part of the exchange, but because our son and his family moved soon after that, we no longer had the same need for the exchange and so are no longer planning to complete it.

Conversely, we owe time to a few exchange partners who we feel are unlikely to do their part of the exchange. Of course, we would love to see them again. Some remain long-distance friends. But after a few years of waiting, we don't really expect them to make the trip to our home.

Is any of this a problem? To us, not at all. Home exchanging has so enriched our lives that we feel we suffer no loss if others have come to our home and we've chosen not to go to theirs. We know others feel the same way.

Monterosso is the largest of the five coastal villages collectively known as the Cinque Terre, located on the Italian Riviera.

How to Choose
a Home Exchange Organization

The first step in home exchange is deciding which home exchange organization(s) to sign up with. The two original home exchange organizations began in the 1950s. Intervac.com was started in Europe by a group of teachers who had a lot of vacation time and were looking for an inexpensive way to travel. All those who joined Intervac.com were provided a listing in a members' catalog which was used to find exchange partners.

HomeLink.org also traces its beginning to the 1950s, when a young high school teacher in New York City named David Ostroff began compiling a list of fellow teachers who had expressed interest in exchanging their houses during the coming summer months. Those lists were distributed and became booklets that gained more and more weight every spring.

This compelling way of sharing homes for vacation grew in popularity, and as time went on, other home exchange organizations were established in a number of different countries. Three of the best known and most successful organizations— Intervac.com, Homeexchange.com, Homelink.org—established sites as the Internet became more widely used in the 90s.

As the Internet became mainstream, these three sites were joined by many new organizations. Today there are at least 50 organizations you can find and consider by doing web searches such as "home exchange" or "home swap". There is a great deal of competition in price, features offered, and number of members. The following are some of the factors to consider in deciding which organization to sign up with:

How Many Listings are on the Website?

The number of listings is very important because that is your universe of potential exchangers and, obviously, the more listings there are, the better your odds of finding a compatible exchange. The number of listings also reflects the number of people who have previously made a decision to join the home exchange organization, presumably after having made the kind of evaluation you will do. Therefore, a large membership may reflect the combined wisdom of the group.

Are you Eligible for a Specialized Organization?

If you are a member of a group for which there is a home exchange organization dedicated to that group, that might be a very good reason for you to join. For example, if you are an educator, you might want to join sabbaticalhomes.com, which is dedicated to academics. If you are a senior citizen, you might be interested in seniorshomeexchange.org. If you are a member of a rotary club, you might be interested in opportunities offered through www.rotary.org. Although these kinds of sites have many fewer listings than the larger sites open to the general public, they may suit your needs because of your membership in the group.

Does it have an Annual Fee or Free Sign Up?

We recommend signing up with an organization that charges an annual fee for several reasons. First of all, an annual fee of around a hundred dollars is not expensive in view of the thousands of dollars you can save through home exchange. Another reason is that paid listings are much more likely to be serious and active exchangers rather than people who just signed up on a whim.

And, finally, the number of listings and features provided by the paid sites are much better in general.

Does the Home Exchange Organization make your Personal Information Public?

Some home exchange organizations publish personal information in listings open to the public including such items as names, addresses, email addresses or telephone numbers. In our opinion, such information should be limited at least to paid members of the organization for privacy and security reasons.

Other home exchange organizations do not disclose such information even to other members. They do this by allowing members to only contact other members through a messaging service they control. Once contact has been made, members can decide for themselves whether to confine their communications to the organization's messaging service or to exchange their own regular email and other contact information.

We usually find it desirable and necessary to exchange our regular email addresses in order to send attachments, since the home exchange sites we use do not support that in their messaging systems. Once we have established communications with our potential exchange partners, we like to provide all our contact information. It is very helpful for exchangers to know the street address, for example, so they can use Google Maps to locate our home and neighborhood and perhaps explore it in street view.

What is the Location of the Listed Homes?

This can be an important factor if there is a particular country you are interested in visiting. Different sites developed in different countries and have large memberships in those countries. If you are looking for an exchange in a particular country, you might want to look at home exchange websites in that country. You can do that for Australia, for example, by doing a Google search for "home exchange in Australia." At present the result of that search is a list that has www.aussiehouseswap.com.au at the top. Browsing its listings, you will see they have about 1200 in Australia and only 12 in the United States. If you live in the US and join their organization, you will have a wide selection of homes in Australia to choose from and at the same time enjoy high visibility with people in Australia who want to visit the US.

What Features does the Website Offer?

Website features include such items as search options with reverse searches to find out who wants to come to your area, filters to limit searches to exchangers who either smoke or don't smoke, have pets, and those who have amenities such as pools, exercise equipment, bicycles or who live in a city center; number of languages supported; types of exchanges available; how listings are presented; and member messaging services.

The appearance of the member listings on the website is important both for presenting your offer and for evaluating other listings. There should be a format which allows plenty of pictures and comprehensive information about the home, the neighborhood and area, and information about the exchangers.

What Support is Provided for Exchanges?

While all the sites are interested in promoting successful exchanges, they differ in the help they provide. Some sites provide guidance such as recommended practices, sample inquiry letters and exchange agreements. Few of the sites are involved in the negotiation of exchanges. In our opinion, that is an arrangement for you and your potential exchange partner to decide jointly, and whatever both parties agree upon becomes the exchange agreement. Several sites offer insurance as part of their service.

Our advice on choosing a home exchange organization is to consider the above factors for any home exchange organization you are considering. As mentioned, you can find numerous home exchange organizations to consider simply by doing a Google search using 'home exchange' or 'home swap' as a search term. We suggest that you evaluate at least several that look interesting to you.

We ourselves are long-time members of two home exchange organizations which we can recommend for your short list of websites to explore: HomeExchange.com and HomeLink.org.

Here is a summary of these two sites:

HomeExchange.com.

As we write this, HomeExchange.com has 46,000 listings in 143 countries, making it the largest home exchange website. It has about 50 team members representing 21 nationalities. The site is available in 16 languages with representatives in those countries available live for questions or to deal with problems.

The website offers a wide range of search options, and the format for listings returned by a search can be either a list or a grid.

In terms of location, you can search by region, country, state or province or other such entity, all the way down to city or town and/or locale including rural, beach or mountain locations.

For listings themselves, you may specify type of home, number of bedrooms and baths, and select from a long list of amenities including wireless Internet, car exchange, swimming pool, and many more.

As for exchange partners and types of exchange, you can limit your search to simultaneous or non-simultaneous exchanges, specify dates, and exclude listings with children, pets, or smokers.

The website also allows you to do a reverse search so you can find out which exchangers have expressed an interest in visiting your area. You can search for listings that have indicated they are available for last-minute exchanges. You may also mark your listing as being available for last-minute exchanges.

You can save any set of your search parameters to use in future searches. You can create a list of favorites and give each a personal ranking so that in planning future trips, you can easily recall and contact them.

HomeExchange.com has made significant changes to its website, adding features that, among other things, focus on improving security, encouraging and facilitating prompt responses to inquiries, and encouraging the documentation of firm agreements between exchange partners.

For example, among improvements to the website's secure messaging system are new features that allow you to politely decline an offer with a single click or, in arranging an exchange, to manage all steps of the exchange process including creating a formal agreement.

HomeExchange.com strongly recommends that as exchange partners get into the details of an exchange, they negotiate and document an agreement. They point out that agreeing to an exchange is a serious commitment, because people make plans, and often buy airline tickets and travel insurance that are non-refundable.

For this reason, the site also provides an exchange agreement form that you can download, fill in with your information, sign and send to your exchange partner. Your exchange partner can then review it, make changes, and return it with his or her signature.

For HomeExchange.com members, the website provides a dashboard that gives you access to edit your listings, edit your account information, and provide exchange reviews. Reviews are feedback that members write describing their exchange experience with each other. The site enables you to post your review and upload photos for members who have confirmed they have completed an exchange with you.

HomeExchange.com feels that the availability of the review mechanism helps maintain a safe, trustworthy home exchange community, encourages information sharing in support of informed decision making, and offers you, the member, the opportunity to build a good reputation as a home exchange partner.

The website provides an extensive help system that explains how to best use the site, how to prepare your listing, how to encourage more inquiries, and various other useful tips and tools.

You can start using HomeExchange.com with their free, but limited, guest pass option. This will allow you to explore the site, search for possible home exchanges, and save your searches. If and when you decide you want to contact other members to arrange a home exchange, you will need to join as a subscribed member. The annual membership fee is presently $119 per year.

HomeLink.org.

HomeLink.org has over 14,000 listings drawn from 78 countries around the world. It has been operating since 1953 and has agents in 27 countries, each of whom is the owner of that country's HomeLink.org organization.

The website has a simple search option and an advanced search option, which only differ in how the search may be qualified. The advanced search option allows you to select the geographic area, type of exchange, dates for an exchange, and to include or exclude a variety of features. These searches are comparable to the searches you can do using HomeExchange.com.

You can also do a reverse search to find out who is interested in coming to your area. The format for the listings returned by the search is a list which can show many listings on a page.

Although the only personal information HomeLink.org requires in their listings is a first name and zip code, it accommodates additional personal information including the address as part of the listing. This enables someone searching for an exchange to locate the exchange home on Google and explore the area. We have found this feature useful in evaluating potential home exchange listings. They do not publish personal email addresses at all, giving members the option to do that or not.

The website has a feature called 'Listing Alerts', which allows you to set up a search with detailed criteria and receive an email notification when a listing appears which meets those criteria. They are currently in the final stage of launching an entirely new search system that will include a natural language search and mapped-based search results.

HomeLink.org operates a messaging system which requires you to initially respond to an inquiry using the system. This allows the website to know how responsive you are to inquiries and it posts the percentages of responses to inquiries as part of each listing. We find this information useful because we believe it tells us something about how an exchanger treats people. We try to keep our percentage at 100% for responding to offers. They also make it easy to send a polite response to turn down an offer with a single click. A planned feature for their messaging system is the ability to include attachments.

The website has what they call a 48-hour hot list, which shows you a list of listings which are new or have been changed within the last 48 hours and a 7-day hot list, which shows you new or changed listings within the last 7 days. This can be helpful in identifying new members or members who have made changes. Either case indicates members who are currently active in seeking exchanges. This system also allows you to get on the list by making changes to get perhaps higher visibility for your listing.

The website also maintains a short-notice list, which indicates members who are seeking exchanges within the next 8 weeks.

HomeLink.org also allows you to maintain a list of favorites and of course to edit your own listing or account information. They have set up an exchange cancellation fund, which is an option in which you can pay a fee to join. This provides some protection if an exchange is canceled by your exchange partner.

HomeLink.org also publishes a newsletter and hosts a home exchange forum for its members.

The annual membership fee right now is $89 per year.

Lanikai Beach is located in the community of Lanikai, a neighborhood in Kailua, on the windward coast of Oahu, Hawaii. Consistently ranked among the best beaches in the world, it has a superb view of the twin islands of Nā Mokulua just off shore.

How to Prepare your Listing

Your listing is very important because it will be the information other members will use to evaluate whether they will want to exchange with you. You want it to make the best impression possible, but of course it is essential that you be absolutely truthful about what an exchanger will experience. As mentioned before, home exchange is based on trust and you never want to do anything to undermine trust.

Develop a List of Features of Your Home and Area

A good starting point for preparing your listing is to develop a list of the things about your home and your area that would appeal to a home exchanger, because you will want to make sure these come across clearly in your listing.

For example, does your home have amenities such as a pool or hot tub, a great view, or appealing outdoor spaces? Does it have many bedrooms, bathrooms? Does it have a well-equipped kitchen? Is there a spacious family room, perhaps with a pool table? Do you have exercise equipment, bicycles or a boat? Do you have good home entertainment facilities?

Do you have a great Internet connection and a computer which exchangers can use? An Internet connection, by the way, is something that has become increasingly important to exchangers even as a telephone has become less important, so you will probably need to have a good Internet connection if you want to interest most potential partners in an exchange with you.

Aside from your home, what activities are available in your neighborhood and the surrounding area? Some of the activities that interest many home exchangers are hiking, biking, golf, boating, swimming, theater and other cultural events, museums, shopping, restaurants, and places of historical interest.

Try to answer with as much detail as you can why someone might want to come stay in your home.

Create a Collection of Pictures for Your Listing

The pictures you include in your listing will probably be the biggest factor that will influence exchangers when they are deciding whether they would like to exchange with you or not.

So once you have developed the list of the appealing features of your home, it's good to consider whether these things can be conveyed in pictures.

You will need to take pictures of your home, both exterior and interior. In this process you will likely begin to look at your home with new eyes and perhaps see a better way to arrange furniture or even to make an improvement in your home. We actually view that as a hidden benefit of home exchange.

Because good pictures are so important to the effect your listing will create, you should give careful consideration to how to do this. If you can afford it, getting a professional photographer to take the pictures could be a good investment.

If you will be taking the pictures yourself, try to use the best camera you can and take a large variety of pictures, varying angles, lighting, and arrangement of accessories. Avoid taking pictures with clutter. Go through all the pictures you take and determine which ones work best.

In the group of pictures, you should include an exterior view of the house, outside spaces and views, amenities such as a pool, and pictures of the various rooms in the house. You can get a good idea of what pictures work well by looking at pictures of other exchange homes on the home exchange websites.

Going back to the list you have developed, think about pictures you can take or obtain of your neighborhood, your larger region, and of the activities available in your area.

It is good if all the pictures are the same size and shape rather than a mixture of shapes and sizes.

Write an Appealing Description of Your Home

Next, you want to provide a written description of your home that explains the things that exchangers will want to know about it such as type of dwelling, number of bedrooms and baths and features of the home.

As mentioned above, if you have a computer exchangers can use, a high-definition TV, a DVD player and a DVD collection, a game machine and games, board games, puzzles, fitness equipment, bikes, kayaks, pool table and other amenities, you should describe those in your listing.

Write an Appealing Description of Your Neighborhood and Area

Provide a written description of your neighborhood and your city or town and the things you like about it. Include activities that are available, cultural events, restaurants, and things that are available in nearby day trips.

Include the distance between your home and public transportation (bus lines, light rails, trains, etc.) in the list of home and vicinity features.

Let People Know Where You Want to Go and When

In your listing, include places you would like to visit on an exchange and indicate whether you are open to offers in other places. Indicate whether there are limitations on the times you can exchange and what those are. Many exchange listings indicate they are open to consideration of all offers and all dates. That will likely bring them more offers, but if there are limitations on the places and times you can travel, you should indicate those.

Introduce Yourself in Your Listing

Finally, include information about yourself to help potential exchangers get to know you. Perhaps include a picture of yourself in your group of photos.

All these things together give prospective exchangers a very good idea of your offer and some information about you. The listings of other members give you, of course, a very good idea of what others offer.

Your listing alone can do a good job of presenting your offer, but many websites also allow a link to a personal website where you can provide unlimited additional information if you wish. So if you have a personal home exchange website, you may be able to include it in your listing. As an example, you can see ours, samandjudyrobbins.us.

If your website allows multiple links from your listing to other websites, you should also consider linking to community websites such as your town's website and websites dedicated to local attractions.

How to Find
Home Exchange Partners

Looking forward to things is half the pleasure of them.

—*Lucy Maud Montgomery*

One of the great joys of home exchange is that you can browse the home exchange offers and take long flights of fancy about what it would be like to visit faraway places, whether they are in your own country or halfway across the world.

You can consider any of the listed options even if they are in very expensive cities because, if you can find an exchange partner, you will have free accommodations and a home kitchen so that you don't have to always eat out in expensive restaurants. Perhaps an exchange car will also be available.

You will find exchange options in one of two ways. Either someone will send you an inquiry or you will send an inquiry to someone where you want to go. Let's look at what happens in both cases:

Someone Sends You an Inquiry

Sometimes, delightfully, you will receive an unexpected exchange request from someone with a marvelous house—say, one with a pool—in a marvelous place—say, south of France—who wants to do an exchange at a time that suits you perfectly. That is wonderful when it happens, but you should know that it rarely happens like that.

One of the things we have learned from our experience both as recipients of requests and as senders of requests, is that home exchange requests have a short shelf life. For one thing, the sender may have sent out a request to a large number of exchangers, so you may be in competition with other people who could also respond.

But even if the request has come only to you, the sender will likely wait just a day or two for a response before moving on to someone else. Therefore, if you receive a request that interests you, you must act quickly. First, you need to seriously think about whether this is somewhere you would really want to go. Look at maps. Look at the climate. Look at attractions and activities in the area. Look at travel costs. Look at the home itself and imagine being there. Whatever the pluses, are there minuses you would find hard to deal with?

Using Google Maps or Google Earth, you may be able to use street views to simulate walking through the streets of the exchange home neighborhood. This is already available for many places in the world and more are becoming available all the time.

We used this tool, for example, to familiarize ourselves with the walk from the metro to our exchange house for a trip to a central city in Europe. When we first used the metro, we knew just how to get to the station and had previewed what we would see along the way.

If the inquiry you're considering is from a place you'd truly like to visit, think about your limitations in regard to when you could go and how long you would want to stay. Would you have the option of a non-simultaneous exchange, or would it need to be simultaneous? If it is advantageous to have a car in that area, would you and that partner be able and willing to do a car exchange?

Are there any showstoppers in regard to this exchange? For example, and very fundamentally, are your available times for an exchange incompatible with their available dates? Or are they smokers and you can't tolerate smoking? Or do they have too large a family to be accommodated in your home? Do they require pet care and you are allergic to pet dander? Unless you plan to travel alone, you and your travel companions will need to make a decision on all these matters together and be able to speak with one voice. Unless everyone is together on the decision, trouble of some kind is likely to lie ahead.

Once you have come to a conclusion, you need to get back to the sender of the inquiry as soon as possible. If you decline, you need to do so in a polite way. If you want to continue the conversation, you will begin what is likely to be an extremely rewarding adventure and a new friendship.

Our involvement in home exchange has made us think a lot about friendship, and it seems to us that shared experiences are perhaps the most common basis for friendship. Whether that is the shared experience of attending school together, working together or exchanging homes, these all have the capacity to create friendly bonds. Sharing the adventures of home exchange and something as personal as your homes just seems to engender friendships.

Sometimes an inquiry will come from someone who lives in a place you have never considered visiting. That has happened to us a few times and led to some remarkable adventures.

Once while we happened to be on an exchange in Hawaii, we received an inquiry from a couple in Australia. Prior to that, going to Australia had not been on our mind, but the inquiry made us start considering it seriously.

Because of that unexpected email, we ended up planning a trip that took us from the east coast to Los Angeles, to Tahiti, to the Cook Islands, to New Zealand, to Australia, to Great Britain and then back home.

This was a trip we would never have contemplated or been able to afford were it not for home exchange.

Another time we received an inquiry from a couple who have a home in La Paz, Mexico, another place we hadn't considered before. The inquiry made us think seriously about whether we would want to go to La Paz, and we decided that, yes indeed, we would be interested in an exchange with them.

We offered them our apartment for the time they wanted and told them we would be happy to come to La Paz at some later time, perhaps on a stopover to or from Hawaii. As it happened, within a few months we received another exchange offer in a place within driving distance of La Paz. We ended up adding a third exchange in that area and altogether, planned a month-long vacation in Mexico.

This is the lesson we have learned from receiving inquiries: although the inquiry may be from a place we have never considered going, we will give it highly focused consideration when we receive an inquiry.

Others will do the same when you send an inquiry.

So if you live in a place that most people don't consider visiting, you can get their focused attention when you make an inquiry. An example of this is the focused attention we gave to an inquiry we once received from someone in a very small town in Denmark. These exchangers indicated they had already done a large number of exchanges, and we honestly didn't understand how they were able to do that until we read their descriptions of the things you could enjoy by being there and all the places you could easily visit from there.

Although we weren't able to actually do an exchange with the family in Denmark, we were very impressed that they made us want to, and their inquiry taught us a lesson that we never forget: There are things to love about your home wherever you live. If you can convey that in your listing and in your exchange inquiries, you have an excellent chance of finding a good exchange partner.

You Send an Inquiry

We strongly recommend that you proactively seek out exchange options rather than just wait for other exchangers to contact you. Depending on where you live and the desirability of your offer, you may find that you will receive a lot of exchange requests, including for places you indicate you want to visit. However, even then, it is unlikely that the requests you receive will be exactly the same ones you would contact if you were selecting the listings.

Option One: Find a Listing Similar to Yours

Keeping in mind that in general you are looking for your counterpart in an area where you would like to visit, you should nevertheless understand that exact parity is not needed. Your home need not be luxurious, for example, if you live in a place like Hawaii, New York City or San Francisco, or near a national park. Potential exchangers with even a luxury home may well be very happy to exchange with you because you live in a place they want to visit.

If you have a family with children, you will probably have greater success arranging an exchange with another family with children than with a couple living in a city. An arrangement with another family with children will likely also offer appropriate bedrooms, toys, books, etc. for each family to enjoy.

You can search for listings similar to yours by using an advanced search for listings which have the same characteristics as your own listing. For example, if you have 5 bedrooms, 5 baths and 4 children, you can limit your search results to listings with those characteristics.

If you want to limit the search results to a particular country or area, you can also do that.

However, based on our experience and the experience of people we know, you should not feel unduly restricted to listings just like yours.

Option Two: Find Exchangers Who Want to Come to Your Area

If your home exchange organization offers it, we recommend that you do a reverse search to find out who in the world may be interested in coming to your area for an exchange.

Because of their interest in your area, you have a much better chance of making an exchange with them than with just a random listing. Looking at those search results is a little like being a guest at a buffet. Let's see now, all these people are interested in an exchange in our area, so where would we like to go?

But there is also an unknown number of people who might want to come to your area but who haven't indicated it in their listing. They may not be thinking about it but would be happy to consider it if an offer is presented to them. For that reason, you should feel free to contact exchange listings as a way to find out if someone wants to do an exchange with you, particularly if they indicate in their listing that they are open to offers.

There are any number of reasons why someone may wish to visit your area. For some people the reason to do a home exchange in a particular area may simply be "I've always wanted to go there for a vacation", but there are other and perhaps even better reasons to choose a destination.

Perhaps someone went to school or worked there in earlier years and still has friends in the area; or perhaps their kids and grandchildren live there, yet as much as they love them, they know a visit can be longer and more relaxed if they have their own place; it may be where a couple fell in love and married and they always talked about it.

31

Or it may be the place from where, way back in time, a great-great-grandparent left to find a better life and thus added a new branch to the family tree; perhaps they have loved reading novels and stories set in a place, or want to go where their much-loved sport or hobby—skiing, quilting, hiking, drawing and painting—would be wonderful to experience. Or sometimes, they just don't really know why, but they're sure they'll find out if they go there.

We too have had exchangers who were motivated by some of these reasons. One of them had a wonderful apartment in the center of Paris, another a home with a private pool in Hawaii and, still another, a beach home in Mexico. We have been very fortunate in having had the opportunity to stay in wonderful places and we know from other exchangers that their experiences with home exchanging have been equally wonderful.

Option Three: Look for an Exchange in Places that Have a Lot of Listings

There are some places that have a lot of home exchange listings. Usually these are very desirable places to live and great places to visit. The large number of listings also indicates that people who live or have second homes there also like to travel. There are hundreds of listings, for example, in Florida, California, Hawaii, and in major cities like New York, Vancouver, and Montreal. There are also large numbers of listings in vacation spots in the Caribbean and Mexico.

Option Four: Look for an Exchange in Places You Want to Go

Another approach is to search for listings in a particular place you want to go. In some cases, there may be very few or no listings on your home exchange website in the area you're interested in, particularly if it's in another country. That doesn't necessarily mean that there are no home exchanges available. Another home exchange organization may have listings for the area and you may be able to search to find out if there is another home exchange website with listings for that area.

Depending on what you find and how much interest you have in that area, you may decide to join an additional home exchange website. That is what we did when we found that HomeLink.org has a lot of listings in Australia, a place where we made two different four-month-long trips by arranging a series of home exchanges in several Australian cities.

Our overall search goal for a given area is to develop a ranked list of our favorite prospects, with our most favorite at the top. We use search parameters to help us develop such a list. For example, we may limit our search to listings that indicate they want exchanges in the US or are open to consideration of all destinations, listings which offer a car exchange, people who are non-smokers and sometimes, people who can do a non-simultaneous exchange. We are particularly interested in listings which offer Internet access and as mentioned before, have noticed that many other people express this as a requirement. If we get a group of listings which have those characteristics, we then look at them carefully for ways to rank the listings in that group.

In some circumstances, we limit our searches to exclude only those characteristics that would be deal-breakers. We don't want to exchange with smokers, we don't want to invite pets, and our home best accommodates only a few people.

If there are many listings, we might also exclude characteristics which are not deal-breakers, but appeal to our biases. For example, we have preferred to exchange with homes that are not primarily rentals because they often are not as well equipped as a home and only rarely allow the owners' personalities to shine through. However, we have also had a number of excellent exchanges with families that also rent their exchange home, so we no longer feel strongly about this.

Many home exchange websites have a feature that allows you to save those listings as a group of "favorites" and provide some way to reflect your ranking of them. That way, you can contact potential exchangers one at a time, working from the top of your list down.

Of course, you could send an inquiry to all the potential exchangers on your list all at once. We do not like to do this because we do not want to receive expressions of interest from more than one family at a time. We would, of course, love to receive an expression of interest from the family at the top of our list, so we first want to find out whether they are interested or not.

We find that out when they either indicate they are interested or not, or when they fail to respond to our inquiry. We allow them a few days to respond and, if they don't, move on to the next family on our list of favorites.

You will find out, as you do this, that not everyone will reply to your inquiry. There are any number of reasons for this. Some people probably don't monitor their email closely, others may not see it perhaps because it goes to a spam folder and, unfortunately, others just don't bother. So, if you don't receive a reply, you need to realize that it isn't personal, and certainly doesn't reflect badly on you. It's just the way things are.

Our philosophy is that we will book an exchange with the first positive response we receive. If someone from a listing that was higher on our list of favorites responds later with a positive response, for us it is not acceptable to backtrack on the first positive responder. So we have to tell the late responder that we already have an exchange arranged.

Although the one-at-a-time, ranked listing approach is our preferred method of contacting potential exchangers, sometimes there is just not enough time to use that approach. For example, for one of our trips to Australia we needed to quickly replace an exchange in one of the cities because our exchange partner had to cancel (this does happen, but rarely). In that circumstance we needed to quickly contact all the potential exchangers in the area. When we did that, we explained the circumstances and informed them all in our inquiry letter what we were doing. We have had to do this twice over the years and in both cases we were able to quickly replace the canceled exchange.

Option Five: Look for Last Minute Exchanges

Another feature of some home exchange websites is a listing of last minute exchanges. This has listings of people who are looking for an exchange in the near future. If you are flexible and want to travel in the near term yourself, you may want to check this list to see if that buffet offers anything interesting.

How to Communicate
with Your Exchange Partners

We recommend that before you begin contacting prospective exchangers, you plan out your whole desired itinerary, particularly if you want to combine more than one exchange in an area. That way, when you begin communicating with prospective exchangers, you have a firm idea of your scheduling possibilities and limitations.

It isn't that you can't change the exchange dates as you enter into communications with exchangers, it's just that you should begin by proposing dates that will work for you. Their responses will then let you know how much leeway you have or need to allow in modifying your plans.

If you do plan sequential exchanges in an area, you will need to consider the activities that will be taking place while you are in each home, how long it will take to get from one home to the next, and if you will want to combine home exchanges with a cruise or a short stay in a resort.

The latter worked well for us when we planned our first trip to Australia. We started our plan with a month-long exchange in a town called Noosa Heads, a resort area where the ocean, Noosa River and Noosa National Park converge. That became our anchor exchange. We then added an exchange in Melbourne in front of that, an exchange in Sydney prior to Melbourne, and an exchange in Lake Taupo in front of that. We wanted to break up our trip to Australia with week-long stops in Tahiti and the Cook Islands. Those were not exchanges.

For the time after our exchange in Noosa Heads, we wanted to spend a couple of days in a resort in Cairns and take a cruise on the Great Barrier Reef for four days. From there we wanted to go on to an exchange in London, and then come back home.

Such a trip as the one described above has to be planned well in advance. If you don't enjoy the planning process and aren't prepared for the need to have a plan B if some part of the trip has to be changed, you may prefer to do simpler exchanges. A single simultaneous exchange has less chance of needing to be changed, and a non-simultaneous exchange is simpler still because only one exchange party at a time is traveling.

For all of our exchanges, we have found the use of an online calendar invaluable both for planning our time and keeping track of our trips and our commitments to exchangers. We use the free Google Calendar which allows you to set up any number of separate calendars, each color-coded, that can be looked at separately, in various combinations, or all together. For example, for us, our blue calendar shows when we'll be away; the red one shows when exchange partners will be in our home(s). Viewing them together helps us make sure we're not planning to be home when exchangers are scheduled to visit or, heaven forbid, that we've double-booked and would have two exchange families, suitcases in hand, at our doorstep!

After you have sketched out a desired itinerary and made a selection of listings of potential exchangers in areas where you'd like to exchange, it is time to begin emailing inquiries. We recommend that you make your inquiry personal, that you use it to effectively and briefly describe the benefits of an exchange with you, and that you make a specific proposal rather than just a vague suggestion of a possible exchange. This is the first opportunity for you and your prospective exchange partners to get to know each other, so it is also good to begin that process by telling them something about yourselves.

You can make your inquiry personal by referring to the prospective exchangers by their names, by highlighting things you have in common, and by commenting on why their home and location are particularly appealing to you. You can convey the benefits of exchanging with you by describing the things you love about your home and your city and some of the things that are available there. And you can make a specific proposal by referring to the itinerary you have sketched out.

Here's an example of a very simple inquiry that might be used:

Dear Charles and Mary,

Your home is beautiful and we would love to do an exchange with you to see how the city has changed since we lived there thirty years ago. We're writing to see if you would like to consider an exchange with us in September of this year. Please take a look at our listing and let us know if you would be interested.

Our apartment is located in an elegant old building in a beautiful downtown residential area in northwest Washington, DC. This location is convenient to public transportation and within walking distance to many shops and restaurants, museums, embassies and the zoo. As you may know, the majority of the museums in Washington are free and there are many historic buildings. There is also a large number of interesting day trips in our area. We are also open to a car exchange.

We look forward to hearing back from you soon,

Best regards,

Judy and Sam

You should keep track of responses as you work through your list of favorites. If no response has been received within a few days, you can go on to the next entry on your list. When you receive a favorable response, you will want to provide your potential exchanger more information about your offer and find

out from them more information about what their ___
provide.

In the exchange of emails exploring aspects of the proposed
exchange, you will both be creating a written understanding of
your agreements, which will serve both of you well. If you find
that the communications aren't working, and that a common
understanding of such agreements as schedule, length of the
exchange, car exchange, pet care, and such are not evolving, and
that trust is also not developing between you, that might be a time
to find a way to politely exit from the negotiations.

Assuming the negotiations go well, as they typically will, there
will be a point when you should summarize the agreements and
send a confirming email of your understandings and ask them to
let you know if you have misunderstood or overlooked anything.

Once the agreements have been confirmed, only the direst
circumstances of illness, death, or other calamity are acceptable
reasons for cancellation of an exchange. If someone does cancel
well in advance, usually other arrangements can be made. To be
prudent, before booking airline or other transportation, you
should ask to confirm again just before you do that to let your
partner know that you are making that commitment.

Another thing you can do to protect yourself against losses on
transportation costs is to take out travel insurance. An easy way to
research available policies is by using online brokers such as
InsureMyTrip.com or SquareMouth.com. Both of these sites have
side-by-side comparisons of various coverages along with prices. It
is a good idea to talk to the insurance provider before making a
decision to make sure that the coverage you are seeking is included
in the policy you select. A website like TravelGuard.com can tailor
a policy to fit your exact circumstances of age, cost of the trip and
other factors.

Some home exchange websites try to encourage members to
avoid misunderstandings between exchange partners by executing

a formal home exchange agreement. Certainly it is important to have a common understanding between the parties, and highly advisable for it to be in writing. But some of the agreement forms we've seen strike a wrong chord with us when they have the feel of contracts and try to address the smallest details that seem to us to fall into the area of common courtesies. For example, we bristle slightly when a form states such obvious things as "Host shall provide clean and tidy premises, including beds made with fresh linens and bathrooms stocked with clean towels." Granted, ours is a personal reaction. Still and all, this is not the kind of contract we would ask a friend to sign, and we prefer to treat our potential home exchange partners as the friends we hope they will become.

We certainly do not advise against using such agreement forms, and if both parties are happy with the way it's done, that's great. If one of our potential exchange partners initiates such an agreement, we are happy to comply and have no problem with it at all, but it's just not something we ourselves would like to initiate.

At the same time, we feel it is very important to have all understandings between exchange partners documented in their email correspondence so both parties have something to refer back to.

Most important, of course, is the basic agreement on dates. This clears the way for us to put our travel dates and theirs on our Google calendar. We'll also want to confirm how many people will be in the party to make sure our apartment can comfortably accommodate them. Sometimes exchange partners will ask if another couple or a grandchild can join them, and again, we have no objection as long as our apartment can accommodate them. If you want to invite additional people to your exchange house, you should cover that in your communications.

Most of the detailed information we provide about our apartment is contained in information sheets we have developed for our exchange partners. These cover such topics as how keys will be provided/located, helpful neighbors, emergency contacts, local and long-distance phoning, trash disposal/recycling, controlling heat/air conditioning, use of laundry facilities and various other appliances, grocery shopping options, restaurant recommendations, and more.

Of course, the information sheet you prepare can and most likely will differ in important ways from those of other exchangers. If you live in a single family house, you may have instructions about resetting the sprinkler, operating the garage door and when to roll the trash cans out to the curb. Plus, whether you live in an apartment, row house or separate house, all homes have unique quirks—advantages and, sometimes, disadvantages—that need to be explained.

Try as we might, we simply have not been satisfied with any generic form we have tried to create, so we modify our form to include specific information for each exchanger. Also, we have found that though it's a good idea to reassure our home exchange partners that this information will be provided well ahead of their arrival, it is best not to send it months ahead as much can change—you have a new house cleaner, you replace your washer and dryer, one store closes and another opens. Better to do the job once—and right—than send a series of potentially confusing versions.

If a car exchange is included in the home exchange, we also create a car exchange agreement like the one at the end of this chapter. This short, but, in our view, important document establishes an understanding of who will pay for parking or speeding tickets, provides insurance information, stipulates that the car will be left clean and with a full tank of gas both at the beginning and end of the exchange, and specifies that if there is an accident, the responsible exchange partner will pay for any loss not covered by the deductible.

As we all know, accidents can happen. To us, being willing to offer a car exchange means also being willing to be prepared for the possibility that our car might be damaged, a camera-recorded speeding ticket might later come in our mail, or a parking ticket might be overlooked. A thorough and thoughtful car exchange agreement helps ensure that a mishap won't sour the exchange experience for either partner.

We find that we get a very good sense of the potential exchangers in our email correspondence. We have encountered, overwhelmingly, wit and charm in their correspondence and in meeting them in person. For whatever reason, it's truly a wonderful community, with very rare exceptions.

However, on occasion, we have encountered potential exchangers who kept bringing up issues we thought we had already agreed upon. This just gives you the feeling that perhaps you don't know what agreements they really have in mind. In such a case, we advise that you find a graceful way to terminate the negotiations.

Although such a case has been rare in our experience, it can happen. For the most part however, you will encounter, as we've indicated, a wonderful group of people.

Another way to help you get to know your exchangers is to talk to them on the telephone. Some people prefer talking on the phone about arrangements and we are happy to do so, but if we do talk about the exchange arrangements on the telephone, we summarize our understandings of our agreements in an email so that both parties can look back to see what was agreed upon.

SAMPLE CAR EXCHANGE AGREEMENT

NAME AND ADDRESS OF REGISTERED OWNER: Samuel O. Robbins & Judith P. Robbins, 9999 California Street, NW, Washington, DC 20008

DATES FOR CAR EXCHANGE: September 1-15, 2010

MAKE, MODEL AND DC TAG NUMBER OF VEHICLE: 2005 Subaru Legacy Station Wagon DC Tag #: 9999

INSURED WITH: State Farm Insurance, Policy Number: 79176-A26-09 Phone Number: 202-999-9999 The car will remain fully registered and insured, with current safety inspection, for the duration of the exchange. The registration and insurance cards will be in the front middle console. A registration sticker is on the front left windshield. The car will be serviced as needed prior to the exchange, left clean and full of gas.

FUEL: Use only Premium gasoline (Octane rating 91 or higher)

IN CASE OF MECHANICAL DIFFICULTIES: Our dealer/service center is Stohlman Subaru in Tyson's Corner, Virginia. If repairs are needed, please call us at your home or on our cell phone: 202-341-9884 to discuss, and provide these numbers to Stohlman as well.

We hereby give _____ permission to be guest drivers of our vehicle. It is understood that they are in possession of valid driver's licenses. They agree to pay for any parking tickets, etc. resulting from their use of the car. In the event of an accident in which an above named guest driver is at fault, he/she agrees to reimburse owners for any deductible/non-claimable part ($1,000) of an insurance claim.

_____/_____

Owners: Samuel and Judith Robbins Date

_____/_____

Guest Drivers: Names and Date

Google Calendar as a Planning Tool

Google Calendar is a valuable trip planning tool which

(1) helps us keep track of our own planned travel;

(2) helps us keep track of commitments we have made to exchange partners;

(3) gives us a place to record other events that will be taking place, such as our housekeeper's schedule, our doctor's appointments, etc.; and

(4) provides us a chronological history of events. This is an excerpt from a trip we took five years ago.

How to Plan Your Trip

O ur two most valuable trip planning tools are Google Calendar and an itinerary format we have developed. The calendar, as mentioned earlier, helps us keep track of planned travel and, most important, of commitments we have made to exchange partners.

Using Google Calendar

Google Calendar is a free time-management web application offered by Google. Like other Google applications, it requires that you have a Google account.

Because it is web-based, you can access it from anywhere using many different types of devices, including PCs, tablets, and smartphones. You can easily share the calendar with family and friends if desired.

You can view the calendar by day, week, or month. For our home-exchange purposes, we most often view a month at a time but it is very easy to change views simply by clicking on another option button. For each calendar event you can include an extended description by clicking on the event edit button.

Google Calendar is integrated with other Google applications such as Gmail and Google Documents. You can open any of those applications from within Calendar by clicking on links.

Google Calendar also has a search feature which enables you to quickly find event entries based on search terms.

We depend on Google Calendar to keep us informed on our

Itinerary as a Planning Tool

DATES	ITINERARY Mexico 2011	ADDITIONAL INFORMATION
Tue, Oct 25, 2011	8:30 am Taxi to National Airport US Airways Flight 662 Washington, DC (DCA) to Phoenix, AZ (PHX) Depart: 10:50am Arrive: 12:40pm US Airways Flight 338 Phoenix, AZ (PHX) to San Jose Cabo, Mexico (SJD) Depart: 01:40pm Arrive: 04:40pm Take free shuttle to Budget Tue, Oct 25, 2011 12:00 PM COL LAS VEREDAS - SJD CARRETERA ENTRONQUE AL APO SAN JOSE DEL CABO, 23400 MX hours Sun - Sat 7:00 AM - 11:00 PM phone 52-624-146-5326 BEST WESTERN Hotel & Suites Las Palmas KM 31 CARR TRANSPENINSULAR San Jose Del Cabo, BCS 23400 526241422131	Travelocity confirmation: 412159229872 Budget car rental Confirmation 41824644US1 Note: Be sure to carry information on Visa coverage and number to call if help is needed at rental counter. Note: It will be too late to drive to Ribera today. Also need to get groceries at Costco in San Jose del Cabo on the way. Stay overnight in motel.
Wed, Oct 26, 2011	Drive to La Ribera – Playa Feliz Lighthouse Point Estates, La Ribera, BCS, MX.	See printed directions to the house from the airport. The house is very close to Hotel Punta Colorado. Manola will let us in the house.
Thu, Oct 27, 2011	Fishing Trip with Victor.	Meet Victor at 7am on the beach in La Ribera
Tue, Nov 8, 2011	Drive to Calle Nicolas Bravo 110 B, e Mutualismo y Madero El Centro, La Paz Baja California Sur, Mexico, 23000	See printed directions to the house. Make sure to take keys on trip.
Tue, Nov 15, 2011	Drive to Villas Baja, Retorno de Golfo, San Jose Del Cabo	See printed directions to the house and instructions to get key.
Tue, Nov 22, 2011	Return rental car and take shuttle to airport San Jose Cabo (SJD) to (DCA) US Airways Flight 333 San Jose Cabo, Mexico (SJD) to Phoenix, AZ (PHX) Depart: 12:40pm Arrive: 02:45pm US Airways Flight 46 Phoenix, AZ (PHX) to Washington, DC (DCA) Depart: 03:55pm Arrive: 09:58pm Taxi to house	

Using this itinerary format as a planning tool has these advantages:

(1) It highlights gaps in your travel plan so you don't overlook making an arrangement such as a need for an overnight stay in a motel enroute.

(2) It puts the details of your trip in one place for your own reference and to easily share with family and friends.

own trip schedules, commitments we have made to exchangers, and as a reference to past exchanges.

The itinerary is a simple three-column document, with the first column simply showing travel dates; the second showing details such as addresses and phone numbers for where we will be; and the third reserved for all the important, varied details—confirmation numbers, ground transportation or rental car information, deposits made and/or amounts due, directions, entry codes, and other such snippets of vital information that accumulate in the travel planning process and, if forgotten, can wreak havoc on otherwise well-laid plans.

Together, these two planning tools have very high value for us. Because our master Google calendar also contains all the details of our everyday, at-home lives, it helps prevent us from committing to an exchange at a time when we need to be at home for medical or dental appointments or for family events—or, our worst nightmare, booking more than one exchange at the same time. The itinerary provides a way for us to easily review our trip plans so nothing has been overlooked; is a convenient way to share plans with friends, family, and exchange partners; and when actually traveling, serves as a handy reference to quickly recall schedules, reservations, and other important information.

Of course, the itinerary is a work in progress and is usually not finalized until close to our departure. Nevertheless, we find it very worthwhile to create it as soon as we have our first snippet of travel information, which often has to do with airline travel.

A Word to the Wise: However firm you feel your commitments with your exchange partner, re-confirm your dates before booking your flights!

ıte resource for researching flights usually starts with
ww.google.com/flights. Its software is used by other
, is very speedy, and is ideal when you want a quick
ʊ.   f possible flights and prices. The only downside is that
you can't buy a ticket on that site.

For comparison you may also want to go to a travel site like
Travelocity.com to see what flights and prices they list—and it's
also worthwhile to do a little more research to find out about
flights that may not be listed on those websites.

One way to find these other options is to look for airlines that
serve airports at or close to your destination. These are often
budget or regional airlines that may not be listed by the major
travel sites. From there, you can then go to the individual airline
sites to find available flights and prices. For example, if you find
that Southwest serves your destination, you can go to
Southwest.com to search flights and buy your tickets.

Also worthwhile can be comparing options at all the airports
that serve your destination, factoring in the availability and cost of
ground transportation. When we used this strategy in planning a
trip to San Miguel de Allende in Mexico, we found that we could
fly to any of three different airports and then take a bus or shuttle
to San Miguel. When we compared the costs of flights to all three
airports, we discovered it was significantly less expensive to fly to
Mexico City and then get to San Miguel using one of the several
luxury but low-cost bus lines that have terminals located right at
the airport. Checking further, we learned on Tripadvisor.com that
many in the American and Canadian expatriate community in San
Miguel swore by that very option. A smooth and scenic ride,
immaculate restrooms, and even a free picnic lunch—what more
could we ask!

Other online trip planning resources we use and you might find
helpful in researching destinations and making your travel
arrangements are yelp.com, fodors.com and frommers.com.

For researching all the attractions of your destination, and
planning what you want to do there, your best resources are most

often your home exchange partners. They are not only very knowledgeable about the area, but also the neighborhood and the very house you'll be staying in.

From their own travels, they know the best way to get to to their home from the airport or train station, the sites, activities and events you would hate to miss, and probably what everything costs. They'll also be your best source of advice on what to do and see right in their neighborhood—the farmers' markets and street fairs, parks and playgrounds, pubs, coffee houses and restaurants that can enhance your enjoyment, however briefly, of living like a local. Plus, they will most likely have lined up friends and neighbors who can help you during your visit.

A good way to begin a conversation with your exchange partners about planning a trip to their home is to provide them with the kind of information they can use in planning their trip to your home.

While our home exchange information sheet includes some information about restaurants, attractions and events right in our neighborhood, it's more of a nuts and bolts guide to living comfortably in our home than an attempt to tell our exchange partners what they specifically might enjoy seeing and doing.

So early on, as we learn more about them and their interests, we do our best to provide them with a steady flow of information about upcoming museum and art exhibits, plays and concerts, fairs and farmers' markets, and other types of regular or special events and attractions that might be of special interest to them.

After the 9/11 attack in New York, citizens in a small town in France had a ceremony in front of the town hall to express solidarity with Americans.

How to Get Your Home Ready
for Your Exchange Partners

When you browse the home exchange listings and see the many attractive and even luxury homes offered for exchange, a natural question to ask yourself is 'Is our house good enough'?

The honest answer to that question is that if you have a well-maintained, clean, and suitably furnished home, you need not worry. One way to think about it is in comparison to a hotel room in your area. A hotel room is expected to be clean and your home of course is also expected to be clean. Beyond that, compared to a hotel room, your home offers much more space, cooking facilities, and indeed all the comforts of home.

As long as you have accurately represented your home to potential exchangers, there should be no problem. They are not looking to buy your home, but merely to use it as a comfortable base for visiting your area. Your exchange partners may have a larger home where they live, but if you live in an area they want to visit, they would have every reason to prefer spacious, free accommodations instead of an expensive, cramped hotel room.

So in getting ready for your exchange partners, at the top of your list is making sure your home is clean, beds have fresh linens, and closets, cupboards and drawers are organized so that your exchange partners can find what they need. They will also appreciate whatever closet, pantry, and other space you can clear so they will have room to hang their clothes and put away the groceries and other things they might buy. This is also a good time to look at your home with new eyes and do things like repair the broken knob on the dresser, clean out the kitchen junk drawer, and perhaps hang a picture on a bare wall. Such changes will not only provide a nicer environment for your exchange partners, they will also be there for your own enjoyment when you return home.

Some home exchangers have a closet or room that remains locked, perhaps to store valuables or personal papers. In our case, it's a spare bedroom closet we have never quite finished organizing. Happily, it always has just enough room for us to a stow a few odds and ends as well as the contents of our hamper before we leave on a trip. On the door, we post a little note that says, "What's in here? Just us skeletons—and stuff Sam and Judy needed to stash at the last minute."

We love to meet our exchange partners whenever possible. Though all our home exchanges have been good experiences, you are likely to find, as we have, that it's the exchange partners you meet with whom you're more likely to establish a lasting friendly bond.

When it happens that we'll be in town when our exchange partners arrive by air or train, we know they're likely to be travel weary. So it's almost always welcomed when we offer to meet them at the airport or station, bring them to our home, and help them get settled in. Plus it gives us a chance to actually show them a few peculiarities of our home—an oddly placed light switch, where a few less used appliances are kept—that are more easily demonstrated than described in writing.

Depending on the time of day, we may also make a pot of coffee or open a bottle of wine and share a simple meal. The only caution is that it's preferable not to tie up your exchange partners too long if they've just arrived after an especially tiring journey. Sometimes, it's better to just greet them, say your goodbyes, and leave them to relax and unwind.

Whether or not we can greet our exchange partners, we always leave a welcoming note on our dining room table where they can't miss seeing it as soon as they arrive. With it are a bottle each of red and white wine, juice or soda if kids are in the group, a box of information about what to see and do in our area, and just in case they forgot to bring theirs, a copy of the Home Information Sheet that was earlier emailed to them. If a car exchange is included in the home exchange, we also leave a copy of the car exchange agreement.

If you are doing successive home exchanges with different sets of exchange partners coming and going while you are away, you'll need help in managing their welcomes and the changeovers. We are fortunate to live in an apartment building and have close friends in the same building who are willing to double check that bed linens were changed, keys were returned, and our house cleaner came as instructed. They are also happy to be the custodians of the wine, snacks and information we have prepared for each new group and to put them out on our dining room table for their arrival.

Whether you live in an apartment building or single family home in the country, if you plan to do successive exchanges, you will want to line up willing and reliable friends, neighbors, or family members to help the changeovers go smoothly when you're away—and to shower them with words and small gifts of thanks when you return home.

Two lorikeets, Georgie and Georgette, came to the kitchen window of our exchange house in Sydney each morning and tapped on it to let us know they were hungry. Here, they sit on the open window sill and eat the bread we gave them.

In Your Exchange Home

When you arrive at your exchange home, you may be greeted by your exchange partners, by friends of theirs, or you may have been mailed a key and emailed any special instructions on how to get into the home.

Typically, when you enter the home, you will be greeted by a welcoming note, instructions on using the various appliances, a collection of brochures and other information about restaurants and things to do and see in the area, and perhaps a bottle of wine and some nibbles. Sometimes there is even a meal to tide you over until you can get to the grocery store.

It's a good idea to email your exchange partners soon after you arrive to let them know you are there and all is well. From our own experience, we know they will be wondering if you arrived safely and if everything is OK. Truth be told, though we all do our best to make everything just perfect for our exchange partners, we are grateful for a few reassuring and appreciative words. This mutual courtesy helps enormously if later in the exchange one or the other partner must rise to the occasion if the house cleaner calls in sick or the air conditioning conks out.

If you are caring for your exchange partners' pet, you need to provide reassurance in that respect, too. In several of our home exchanges we have had a much-loved cat to care for. In fact, over time we have encountered many cat personalities and enjoyed them all. Most important, we have learned that of all the things absent pet-owning exchange partners are concerned about, though they may not mention it, is how Fluffy or Mittens is faring. Having had pets ourselves, we understand. So within the first few days of our arrival, we do whatever we can to make friends with our exchange pets so we can take pictures showing how well they've adjusted to these strangers who have invaded their turf. When we send the pictures to our exchange partners, the reaction is magic. Their sighs of relief can almost be heard in the messages they email back to us.

You will need to plan time to clean your exchange house before you leave. We aspire to leave it at least a little better in some way than it was when we came, and have heard from others that this is a typical sentiment. It's simply that the psychology of exchanging versus renting a place is so different. In exchanging, you feel like a friend has done you a great favor, which is true, and you are grateful and want to reciprocate.

Before you leave you will need to replace any food items or supplies you have used and to communicate with the owners if you have broken any objects. You will be responsible for either replacing them or reimbursing the owners. You will also want to make sure that you will be taking care of any home security or other matters according to the owner's instructions.

It's a good idea to send an email when you're leaving or soon after to let your exchangers know you've left and that everything is OK.

Finally, before you leave, it's a good practice to write a thank you note and to leave your hosts a small house gift.

After You Return Home

When you return home you are most likely to find your home neat and clean, as this is a common basic trait of exchangers—to leave the exchange home in at least as good condition as they found it. Usually there will also be a thank-you note and perhaps a small house gift.

It is not unusual though to find that some things are in slightly different places, such as dishes, pots and pans, bed pillows, even chairs. That is because your exchangers were not able to remember exactly where you keep everything, and simply put them back where they thought they belonged. Easily forgivable, because you will do the same kind of thing in your exchange homes, no doubt. And if your exchangers had an early flight, you may find used linens in your hamper instead of washed and dried. In such a case, they will have already made such an arrangement with you and if you leave an extra set of clean sheets, they will have been able to remake the beds prior to their departure.

We recommend that you send an email to your exchangers soon after your return home to thank them for taking good care of your home and for any note or gift they may have left for you. We know we are grateful to receive such an email from our exchangers.

In most cases, by this time you will likely feel a friendship toward your exchangers and you will want to continue some kind of a connection, perhaps even extending to exchanging with them again sometime in the future and getting together if your paths happen to cross.

One way to continue the friendship is to continue corresponding by email, sharing pictures and experiences from your trip. We like to use photos and video from our travel to create photo shows on photoshow.com. We also send our end-of-year holiday letter which summarizes our year not only to friends and family at home, but also to our exchangers. Some exchangers will respond to that by sending us updates on their adventures and perhaps their own end-of-year letters. Some friendships, as we've described, develop into longer-term friendships in which we exchange emails commenting on events in the exchangers' country, reports from their travels, and meeting up with them in other places and spending time together.

By the time you've gotten to know your exchangers through correspondence, meeting them, and sharing the intimacy of your homes, a friendship sometimes naturally develops. That doesn't happen in all exchanges for a variety of reasons, but when it does, it's very rewarding and it's something you usually don't get when you travel and stay in hotel rooms.

Both of the home exchange organizations we belong to, HomeExchange.com and HomeLink.org, recommend that both exchange partners complete an exchange evaluation upon their return from an exchange. Normally these reviews will be positive and clearly, glowing reviews can benefit a listing.

Over the years we have expressed our positive feelings directly to our exchange partners and frankly not thought much about entering reviews in the home exchange organization websites, and most of our exchange partners have done the same.

But because reviews are becoming much more widely used in recent years on many different kinds of websites, home exchange reviews seem to be becoming more important, too.

We now believe that providing reviews probably offers a good way for you to establish an excellent reputation by gaining positive reviews for your listing.

You can do that by first, providing an excellent home exchange experience for your exchange partners, and second, by providing a positive review for your exchange partner. That is likely to inspire a positive review for your own listing.

So, Is Home Exchanging
Right for You?

By you, we mean you and yours—the spouse, family, friends and other dear ones who will be part of a home exchange. It's a question only you and they can answer.

It's a key question because, despite its many benefits, home exchange may not be right for everyone. A lot depends on temperament and circumstance. While circumstances can be in flux, temperament rarely budges. A case in point, among our friends is a couple who could never reach a meeting of the minds about the concept of home exchange. For him, it's less a matter of "What about my stuff?" than a deep-seated aversion to the idea of anyone he doesn't know sleeping in his bed or perusing his bookshelf. For her, the reaction is to smile, shrug, and plan a trip they can both enjoy. She knows he'll never change.

But as we said, circumstances do change. For a stressed-out working couple in dire need of a vacation—whose present idea of a vacation is a relaxing, pampered week at a resort—the idea of going to an unfamiliar home, however lovely, and doing any household chores, may be none too appealing. Not now at least. But after the baby comes? The idea of a nice exchange home at the beach, with a nursery and all their exchange partners' baby equipment, may feel like the perfect vacation solution.

As a family grows, the idea of home exchange can seem both more enticing and yet more challenging. The prospect of spending nothing on accommodations but having more room to spread out, plus the possibility of bicycles, toys, games and sports equipment when exchange families are similar, sounds wonderful. But for big, busy families, getting a home ready for exchange partners can be a showstopper. Our suggestion is to estimate the amount of money that, without a home exchange, you'd need to spend on hotels, possibly a rental car, and lots of restaurant meals. Then use part of it for some improvements, if needed, to get your home exchange-ready, and the rest for cleaning services. True, this strategy won't clear all the clutter, but there's always the basement or a spare closet or room, and you can take comfort in the thought that your exchange partners are probably a family with challenges much like your own.

If your nest is empty, particularly if you are retired, with home exchange the world can be your oyster—if you wish it to be. If you are happy and content with your life just as it is; if you could not imagine leaving friends and family, however briefly or rarely; if you have seen all of the world you had hoped to see, you are truly blessed. By all means stay put, knowing that should adventure call, home exchange offers you another way to respond.

Even if you are intrigued with the the concept of home exchange, and even though the experience of the vast majority of home exchangers is overwhelmingly positive, it's not unreasonable to ask:

Can Anything Go Wrong?

It would be entirely unfair and untrue to say anything but yes, of course it can. Things can go wrong in the process of trying to arrange an exchange and in the exchange itself. Here, from our own experience and that of other home exchangers we know are some of the common things that go wrong and what you can do about them.

1. You've set up your home exchange website listing and you don't receive any inquiries.
It's possible you haven't done as much as you could do to provide information and, through words and pictures, make your

listing sufficiently appealing. Experienced home exchangers tend to look not only at what is in a listing but also what isn't. So if, for example, your home has three bedrooms, better to show them all than have people wonder why you didn't. Also, if you live in an area less known for tourism, you need to do an extra good job of presenting your offer and then making inquiries yourself rather than just waiting for offers to come to you.

2. You've made inquiries and you either don't receive a reply or receive only negative replies.

Unfortunately, there are some people who just don't bother to respond. Perhaps they're presently unable to do exchanges, or are in a popular destination and feel inundated with inquires. Do understand, we are not making excuses for anyone. We feel that every inquiry deserves a response. But if you don't hear back within a day or two, don't stew, just move on to the next prospect on your list. You'll also find that you receive more negative than positive responses. But that's OK. You only need one that is positive, and you, too, will decline more offers than you accept.

3. You've connected with a potential exchange partner, but despite copious emails, the two of you just can't seem to reach an understanding.

Once in awhile—but fortunately not often—it happens. You begin to doubt if a mutual commitment exists; worry that issues that seemed settled keep coming up again; or you just generally have an uneasy feeling.

If you find that you're not able to communicate easily and effectively with a prospective exchange partner and establish a friendly rapport within a reasonable time, we advise you to trust your gut and find a polite way to terminate the discussion. The vast majority of home exchangers are very easy to communicate with, and where genuine interest exists, understandings tend to come quickly.

The most successful home exchanges are those that feel like a win-win early on, with enthusiasm on both sides. If either is lacking or halfhearted, it's almost always better to part ways and look for another exchange partner. Better to move on than find yourself with non-refundable plane tickets you can't use.

4. After your initial agreement, your exchange partner asks for changes or new conditions.

Your response will probably depend on what's being asked, how you deal with change in general, and how important this particular trip is to you. Home exchanges are usually scheduled months in advance, during which life goes on. Your exchange partners might ask about bringing another couple or doing a car exchange after all. Ideally, such issues are best settled early on, and our advice—in the spirit of home exchange and the golden rule—is to be accommodating if you can.

On the other hand, if you have stipulated in your listing that no one will smoke or bring a pet to your home, these would most likely and understandably be deal breakers regardless of your desire to visit the exchange location.

5. Your exchange partners inform you just prior to the exchange that they will be unable to do the exchange for medical or other pressing reasons.

This regrettable situation does arise, though rarely. When it does, all you can do is work out another plan, and often your exchange partner will help you find an alternate solution. But if not, you may be able to find another exchange on short notice. As a rule, you'll find that the home exchange community is very sympathetic to such situations and will want to help, and those with second homes are particularly able to do so.

6. You're on a home exchange when in the exchange home an appliance stops working, the brakes go out on the

car, or something else needs attention now.

The usual understanding is that the owner will cover the expenses for utilities and necessary household maintenance and the visiting exchanger will pay for any damage they themselves cause. Typically, exchange partners will leave instructions on what to do/who to contact when such things go awry, and in many instances, ask that you contact them as well. If you cause any damage you should notify the owner and make it clear that you will pay for the damage. If it's an instance of breaking an everyday item like a wine glass, your exchange partner will most likely tell you not to worry about reimbursement. He knows he may well break one of yours.

7. You're on a home exchange when your exchange partners calls or emails to tell you they've broken a lamp or had a mishap with your car.

If you just put yourselves in their shoes, you'll easily be able to imagine how terrible they must feel and what a pall it could put on what was supposed to be a pleasant experience. So the kindest thing you can do is to reassure them that what happened to them could have happened to anybody, and urge them not to let it spoil their trip.

This will be easier for you if, in arranging the exchange, your understanding includes how such an event will be handled. With car exchanges, it is commonly agreed that, in the case of an accident, reimbursement will be made for the deductible amount if repairs are needed. The balance of your losses will be reimbursed by insurance, and while you may suffer some inconvenience, it shouldn't affect the good relationship you want to maintain with an exchange partner.

8. You arrive home to find that some things are not in their proper place, your home hasn't been properly cleaned, or something valuable is missing.

That things will have been moved around a bit is a given because your exchange partners simply won't remember where you keep everything. Among a kitchen's most migratory items are the scissors and the corkscrew. Look in the other drawer.

If your exchange partners don't leave your home as neat and clean as they found it when they arrived, they need to learn to do better. If it really bothers you, rather than stewing, resolve to get in a house cleaner before you return from your next home exchange.

On the other hand, if something valuable is missing, or your personal papers seem disturbed, that indicates a serious—and thankfully, in the world of home exchange, unlikely—problem. But for your own peace of mind, you may want to consider putting small valuables and certain papers in a locked closet or other secure place before you leave home.

9. Something comes up on your side after an exchange has been agreed upon that makes you want to cancel the exchange.

Seasoned home exchangers know that it is incumbent on them to fulfill commitments that they have made. If a cancellation of an exchange is absolutely necessary after airline tickets, other exchanges linked to yours, and other arrangements such as theater tickets have been made, most regretful exchange partners will make heroic efforts to provide alternative arrangements, perhaps even at their own expense. If you are not willing to honor your commitments in this spirit, home exchanging may not be right for you.

Knowing these things can happen, you may just prefer to rent, if you can afford to, when you travel, just so you don't have to consider the possibility of having to deal with any potential exchange problems.

The Bottom Line

In this book we have attempted to cover both the advantages of home exchange and the possible disadvantages. As we have noted, both of these can vary with a family's available time, circumstances, and inclinations.

For us and many others, the relative inconveniences of home exchange are greatly outweighed by the opportunities to travel widely, stay longer and enjoy new friendships. After all, there is a fair amount of work involved in arranging ordinary travel, and it costs a great deal more. Home exchangers as a group seem to be people who enjoy making new friends.

So if you have a home to offer, like to travel, have time to do it and enjoy meeting new people, our recommendation is to try it. It's not expensive to do and the potential rewards are great.

Kangaroos in Murramarang National Park feed as the sun goes down.

Four Months Down Under

This giraffe in the Sydney zoo has a million-dollar view of the Sydney skyline.

A Travel Narrative

We had already done a fair number of home exchanges prior to our first trip to Australia in 2003. We had never before considered traveling to Australia at all, but while we were on an exchange in Hawaii in 2002, we received an inquiry from an Australian couple that made us start thinking about planning a trip there.

We ended up planning an around-the-world trip with stops in Tahiti, the Cook Islands, and a series of home exchanges in New

Zealand, Australia and London. We supplemented our home exchanges with short stays in paid accommodations in Tahiti, the Cook Islands, Auckland, Wellington, Christchurch and Cairns, where we also went on a short cruise on the Great Barrier Reef.

We loved the people, the countries, and our experiences so much that we had to go back in 2008. This is our account of that second trip from notes we made during the trip.

Koalas are native to eastern Australia, where they live in and feed on eucalyptus trees. They are classified as marsupials, mammals which carry their young in a pouch for the first months of the youngsters' lives.

Journal Entries from Our Second Trip to the Land of Wonders

FRIDAY, JANUARY 18, 2008

Bula!

Main Street of Levuka.

On Tuesday evening, we boarded a 10:30 pm flight from Los Angeles to Fiji on Pacific Air, Fiji's national airline. Crossing the dateline, we would lose a day, so as night slowly dissolved into dawn, we made landfall early Thursday morning. The first thing we noticed about Fiji we noticed from a thousand feet up: below us was every shade of green, from the near black of staid colonial shutters to the young upstart brightness of a Granny Smith apple. The patterns were not blocks and grids as measured, plowed, and planted by man, but rather swirled and splattered across the land by the exuberant hand of nature.

The second thing we noticed about Fiji was the rain (which should not have been a surprise given all the green!). From the moment we landed, rain was either approaching in the gray bellies of fast-moving clouds, cooling us with a refined mist, or pelting us with oafish splatters in a run-for-cover deluge before moving out to sea to make way for the sun.

Our plane had arrived in Nadi, Fiji, around 5:30 am and we knew we faced a busy day to get to our first destination—Levuka on the smaller neighboring island of Ovalau, which can only be reached by one boat or plane a day. First, we took a bus, the Queen's coach, across the island of Viti Levu to Suva, where we were scheduled to arrive at noon. Then we needed to get to the ferry landing, about an hour and a half's drive from Suva. Believing the ferry left at 2:00 pm, we asked a taxi driver if we could make it, and he said that it would be tight, but he would hurry, and could probably make it.

So off we went. Only later did he mention that he was newly to Fiji from India and had never been on the road we were to take, much less to the ferry landing! A cyclone somewhere far offshore was bringing a driving rain. The road was very rough and full of potholes, which our driver mostly avoided by weaving and dodging up the rain-slicked road at death-defying (or so we fervently hoped) speed, and we arrived with twenty minutes to spare. Only then did we learn that the ferry would not actually leave until "the bus arrived from Suva" (which we realized we could have taken!). Ah well. The bus was early. The ferry ride was lovely. We arrived in

Levaku around 6 pm, checked into the old Royal Hotel, and collapsed.

"Bula" is the all-purpose Fijian word for hello, welcome, good to see you, and in actual translation means "health." We heard it and said it dozens of times from the moment we arrived in Levuka, which is pretty amazing, because Levuka is a very small town on a very small island.

Nevertheless, it was the capital of Fiji back when the only way to get to this island nation was by ship. Levuka, unlike the larger islands, was blessed with a sheltered, east-facing harbor, which was a necessity when copra was king and ships came from around the world to collect it and the lesser products such as the pearl buttons for which Levuka was famous. But even in the town's heyday, when ships filled the harbor, grand houses sprouted on the hillsides, and the lure of bars pressed cheek to jowl along Beach Street kept every seaman pulling his weight, it was clear that Levuka could not remain the capital of Fiji for long. With the sea to its front and high mountains to its back, there was no room to grow. So eventually the capital and all its trappings of bureaucracy were moved to Suva on the larger island of Vitu Levi. In the ensuing years, as the copra trade hit hard times, plastic buttons replaced pearl, and the harbor emptied of ships, little Levuva went to sleep.

Today, for all the change Fiji has undergone—ceded by its chiefs to the British Crown in 1879, and made independent again in 1970, with a dramatic rise in tourism—Levuka sleeps on. We came here because Judy was seduced by its description as the only place in the South Pacific that today would still feel like home to the likes of Somerset Maugham. But once we arrived, we both fell in love with Levuka.

Our hut on a small island was built and owned by Fijans. On one of the days we were there, we visited them on another small island where they live.

THURSDAY, JANUARY 24, 2008

Barefoot Island

Fijian crew singing and playing as we head toward our island village on Barefoot Island.

At the last moment, on the day we were scheduled to leave Levuka, fly to Viti Levu and spend a night in Suva, we learned that our flight had been canceled. The cyclone that had been intermittently pelting us with rain had prevented our plane from taking off from another island to come to ours. While this meant that we would not be able to see Suva, the present-day capital of Fiji, it did mean that we would be able to have one more dinner at our favorite restaurant in Levuka and stay one more night in our little cottage at the Royal Hotel. Not a bad outcome, especially when it would all be paid for by the airline. By the next morning, the weather had cleared, and a taxi took us to the little airport on Ovalau—where *we* were weighed along with our luggage! Rather than flying to Suva, we took a direct flight to Nadi, from where we would leave the next morning on our three-day, two-night Sailing Safari offered by Captain Cook Cruises.

The Captain Cook staff picked us up the next morning and took us to our boat, a 108-foot square-rigged topsail schooner which had originally been commissioned by a generous benefactor for the youth of New Zealand. When the benefactor's trust later commissioned a replacement to be built, Captain Cook purchased the older boat. In addition to us, our group included two forty-something couples from British Columbia, a young New Zealand couple who were expecting their first baby in June, a British couple about our age, a family of four from Reno, Nevada, a boyfriend and girlfriend from the Netherlands, a single mom from Australia traveling with her son and the young woman who rented her "granny flat," and a native Fijian couple who lived in Sydney and had last been home for a visit three years earlier.

By 9:00 am we had left the dock in Nadi and were on our way to the Captain Cook village, Barefoot Island—aptly named as it occupies the tiny island of Drawaqa in the Yasawa Group northwest of Viti Levu, and is known for its natural beauty and excellent diving and snorkeling. After seven hours, with one snorkeling stop on the way, we arrived at our destination, Barefoot Island. The entire island of Drawaqa is leased to the company by a nearby Fijian native village, and the company has done an admirable job of designing their modest resort to resemble a traditional village. On arriving, we settled into our little thatch-roof hut called a *bure*, grabbed our snorkeling gear and took a first look at the reefs that were practically outside our door. The turquoise water was "high definition" clear; the coral was wonderfully healthy; and the fish created a kaleidoscope of color.

The next morning we took an early morning hike up to the highest ridge on our little island. We were led by "Bio," an exceedingly hospitable and patient native Fijian whose title seems best described as "cruise director," and accompanied by the island dog, "Seta." It was an easy hike, no more than an hour, and with gentle climbs. But from the highest point, we could see across the channel where thousands of Manta Rays make their annual migration, and across which Seta swims often enough to have fathered many litters of puppies on the neighboring island. After our hike, we were ready for breakfast, and later for the job of planting our own banana tree. Every individual, couple, family, or group that comes to the island is given the opportunity to plant a coconut palm, papaya tree, or banana tree to help "green" the environment and feed future visitors—or themselves, if they're fortunate enough to return in the future.

Of course, every village needs a chief and a spokesman. Sam had the honor of being the chief for the entire three days, and his primary responsibility was to lead the Kava ceremony. Kava is the root of a plant much favored by Fijians for its mild mellowing effect. It is harvested, dried, ground into a powder, poured into a cloth bag, mushed around tea-bag fashion in a large wooden bowl, and then doled out with great ceremony in small cups fashioned from coconut shells. A practice ceremony was held our first night on Barefoot Island in preparation for our next-day visit to a true Fijian village, where we would participate in a Kava ceremony led by the village elders. When offered a cup, we all performed the ritual—clap once with cupped hands, say "Bula," drink, clap three more times—without a hitch. This was followed by lots of dancing, first by the villagers, then with all of us joining in, and later with a low-key, no-pressure opportunity to support the village by purchasing locally made crafts. Coming back to Barefoot Island from the visit to the village, the sail was raised on the boat and the quiet ride, along with the singing and playing of ukulele and guitar by our Fijian guides, created a wonderful sail back.

That night, our last night, each country was urged to present a "show" for the entertainment of all. Sam and Judy, accompanied by the Fijian musicians, represented the U.S. by demonstrating American swing dance. Almost everyone gamely came up with something, and everyone was declared a winner.

From Bio and others of the amazing crew and staff, we learned that the village structure is very much alive in Fiji. Even on the largest island of Viti Levu, which Fijians refer to as "the mainland," most people either live in a village or maintain close ties to their home villages on more distant, less-developed islands. Typically, the village is peopled by a kinship clan of families living in small cement block houses with corrugated roofs or sometimes, even today, in traditional bures. When the elders in a family pass on, they are laid to rest in front of the home in graves marked with large cement markers shaped like beds, and the home passes to the next generation. Central to each village is a larger main bure, more often of traditional style, which serves as church, community center, and recreation hall. Because the village school usually only goes through the primary grades, the children must go to the mainland to continue their education. There they board with other families during the week and return to the village on holidays and weekends.

Every crew and staff member had come from a village on one of the smaller islands, and left his village to pursue a secondary education in Suva. Particularly since the recent non-violent coup in Fiji—a result of the ongoing tensions between the native Fijians, who have full rights, and the large minority of immigrants from India, who have lesser rights—good jobs have been hard to come by in Fiji. The men who sailed our ship, cooked our meals, and in their non-working moments made beautiful music with instrument and voice, were to a man overqualified for the work they were doing. We all knew this, but we all knew as well that there was little we could do other than express our appreciation as individuals, one on one, and contribute with special generosity to the gratuity they would share.

As we took our leave on the last day, we passengers talked among ourselves about how the experience far exceeded our expectations. But really, that is a gross understatement. In truth, none of us had felt we had the right to expect the open hearted, warmly accepting friendship extended to us by the Fijian people we met, but we were deeply grateful to have received it.

TUESDAY, FEBRUARY 12, 2008

Canberra

Canberra with the large flagpole on Parliament in the middle.

From Fiji, we had a too-short stopover in Auckland, New Zealand, before we flew to Sydney and then took the train to Canberra. Ever the thrifty travelers, we had chosen the train instead of flying from Sydney to Canberra because of the much lower cost, and fortunately the convenient rail link from the Sydney airport to the central train station made it an easy decision. Sydney's central rail station is a grand old building with cathedral-like ironwork overhead that makes it light and airy in feel. Housed in the station is a very enticing museum chronicling the history of Australia's rail system. But because we were traveling on a Sunday, it was closed, so to see it, we would have to wait until we would be staying in Sydney instead of just passing through.

The train ride was a revelation for both its scenic beauty and its efficiency. Our train was no youngster, and would never be mistaken for its flashy European or even American Amtrak cousins. But it was clean and comfortable and serviced by a friendly crew of older men and women who made the trip a pleasure. About halfway through the journey, a well-padded motherly attendant came through the car announcing that a "hot meal" was available, the choices being roast lamb with vegetables or curried chickpeas. Sam opted for the roast, and enjoyed it while watching the passing scenery, which, except for the stands of exotic-to-us gum trees shading the herds of grazing cattle, reminded us of the great plains of the American west.

Along the way we stopped at numerous small towns, each with its own Carpenter Gothic Victorian railroad station painted in the dusky red and gold colors typical of Australia's 19th century public buildings. Under the long covered gallery fronting each station were bright blue wooden benches, standing in a row, with the station name stenciled in large white letters. Arriving in Mittagong, Bundanoon or Bungendore, it often felt as if you were stepping into the set of Neville Shute's *A Town Like Alice*, albeit after the heroine had spiffed things up.

In Canberra we were met at the train station by our friends and exchange partners, Wayne and Judy Ryan, who had the past summer visited our city home in Washington, DC, and our country home in the mountains near Lexington, Virginia. Wayne and Judy had generously offered to host us in their home for a few nights and show us around Canberra before we moved on to their beach house on the coast of New South Wales in Broulee. Canberra was shrouded in clouds for most of our visit, but it was still interesting seeing the capital city of Australia, so different from our own.

Whereas the monumental center of Washington, DC, was the vision of a Frenchman infatuated with the grand circles and radiating boulevards of 19th century Paris, Canberra realizes the more modern and unique vision of an American architect, Walter Burley Griffin, who in 1911 won an international competition to design the new Australian capital. In designing Canberra, Burley had a nearly blank slate. The site for the new Australian capital was carved out of the sparsely populated country between Sydney and Melbourne—an expedient choice when it became clear that the two cities could not end their incessant bickering as to which deserved to be the capital.

Canberra's natural centerpiece is a large artificial lake stretching the width of the city center, its northern edge broken by several peninsulas that reach almost to the southern side, where the monumental centerpiece is the new Parliament Building, built in 1988. But the city itself stretches well beyond these points, and includes four distant and distinct satellite towns. Were Washington, DC, as large, these four satellite cities would be as removed from the center as are some of DC's more distant suburbs, but with mostly picturesque countryside rather than subdivisions, strip malls and crowded highways in between.

Viewed from the outside, the Parliament Building rises out of the ground, forming a hill that is part building and part wide green walkways perfect for strolling or for rolling down, were you a child or feeling like one. Inside are housed all the offices one would expect in a place where hundreds of politicians and lawmakers served by hundreds more staff go about their daily work. But the offices are well hidden, and it is the soaring open spaces, fashioned from native materials—gleaming marble of many colors, burnished woods of every description—and the evocative tapestries and paintings displayed within them that make it truly a building of and for the people of Australia. Days later, as we watched the historic events unfold in Canberra with the Australian Parliament's historic declaration of apology to the Stolen Generations of aboriginal people, we felt especially grateful that we had been given the opportunity to visit the building where those events took place.

On our last night in Canberra, Wayne and Judy invited her sister, Barbara, Barbara's husband Chris, and friends Kerry and Digby to dinner. It was a lovely time in lovely company and reinforces our view that friends sharing friends with other friends is the ultimate generosity.

An encounter with kangaroos in the background and 'kangaroos' in the foreground
while on a morning walk with Wayne and Judy near their house in Canberra.

SATURDAY, FEBRUARY 16, 2008

Melbourne

Our group having pho for lunch in Melbourne.

Though we had fallen in love with the city on our earlier trip to Australia, Melbourne was not on our itinerary this time. But after arranging our home exchanges, we learned that two of our sons, Eric and Ian Hilton, were going to be in Melbourne during our time in Australia, and we just had to arrange to be there too.

Thievery Corporation, the music group headed by Eric and his friend and business partner, Rob Garza, had agreed to play in the multi-city Good Vibrations Music Festival, which was scheduled to kick off in Melbourne on February 9. Ian, then chief executive officer of an international website development company, needing to visit several far-flung company offices, including Melbourne's, had scheduled his stop there to coincide with the festival. Learning all this, we quickly dashed off an email to our friends and previous exchange partners in Melbourne, Richard and Kerry Martyn, who graciously said yes when we asked if they might put us up in their home for a few days.

Richard and Kerry had been living in Noosa Heads in Queensland when we had exchanged with them in 2003. Meeting them and staying a month in their Noosa Heads home had been two highlights of our first trip to Australia. Though they had since spent time in our DC apartment and our country home, it had been when we were traveling, so it was wonderful to be able to meet up with them again years later, and see their new home in our favorite neighborhood of Melbourne, North Carlton.

Melbourne covers a very large geographical area, with what would be considered inner city neighborhoods many miles out from the center. But North Carlton, an area of Victorian terrace dwellings of all sizes—from grand mansions once occupied by the city's movers and shakers to tiny three-room houses occupied by their servants—is just a few tram stops from Melbourne's central business district. After World War II, North Carlton became home to the huge wave of Italian immigrants that came from Calabria, and today all of Melbourne delights in the feast of Italian restaurants that line Lygon Street, one of the neighborhood's main thoroughfares.

Richard's and Kerry's North Carlton home is a "beaut," as Aussies tend to say when speaking in the superlative. Like most of the Victorian terrace houses, it is one story, sitting low on its bit of ground and close to the sidewalk, with a covered front porch embellished with fanciful ironwork and, over the front door, a stained-glass transom announcing its name—in their case, Mayville. These names were chosen not by the people who first occupied the homes, but by the people who built them with such pride and skill more than a hundred years ago. Inside, Richard and Kerry's home is bright, airy, and open, with every bit of space

82

inside and out used to maximum advantage. Anyone contemplating a home makeover would do well to stand on their shoulders.

On our first night in Melbourne, Richard and Kerry had graciously invited our gang to dinner. It was a jolly group: Richard and Kerry, the two of us, Eric and his wife Tien, Ian, and Frank, a delightful and talented musician who was performing with Thievery at the festival.

The food was delicious, and the meal was capped by an enormous Pavlova—a specialty of Kerry's. This festive Australian dessert is comprised of a baked meringue topped with fruit and whipped cream, and is intended to be rather light unless you eat as much as we did!

The next day, once again with Richard and Kerry, Eric and Tien, Ian, and Frank, it was off to Richmond, the Vietnamese section of Melbourne to feast on pho and wander the shops and market stalls that line this lively neighborhood. Later, we all went our separate ways, with the two of us walking for miles and rediscovering much that we love about Melbourne. That evening, Richard and Kerry joined us for dinner at a darling Asian restaurant in North Carlton, and then it was early to bed in anticipation of the next day's festival.

We suppose a proud mom and stepdad would be forgiven for going on overmuch and with an excess of superlatives about finding themselves halfway around the world and witnessing one dear son performing on the stage and another standing down front where he could be seen in silent, ever-present support. For parents, it's more than a "Dear Diary" moment, it's a "Thank You, God" moment—thank you for endowing them with gifts for which we can claim no credit, and for safely carrying them through and beyond our errors and oversights to this wonderful, absolutely unforgettable day. For concert goers who might have noticed her, there was no need to worry about the woman looking down from a high balcony, who occasionally touched the corners of her eyes with a tissue. It was just the irrepressible expression of a mother with a grateful heart.

Immediately after the show, Eric and Tien, with the twenty or so others of Thievery Corporation, had to leave for Brisbane, where the second in the series of four festival concerts would take place the next day. But Ian had a bit more time in Melbourne, and so was able to come with us and Richard and Kerry for a trip down memory lane—dinner at Café Coretto.

Of all the dozens of Italian restaurants along Lygon Street, this was the one we had designated as our favorite on our earlier home exchange in Melbourne. At least once a week, and sometimes more, we would take a table on the sidewalk and order the same thing——pizza, veal Parmesan with spaghetti Bolognese, and a half liter of house red. Now, five years later, we were back for more of the same. One always risks disappointment on returning to a place writ large in memory. But not this time. Even more than the pizza, which was as good as ever, the reward was in the company and the rich cache of new memories that would sustain the glow of our four days in Melbourne.

FRIDAY, FEBRUARY 22, 2008

Broulee

Our resident crimson rosellas on the balcony at Wayne's and Judy's apartment at Broulee.

Wayne's and Judy's house at Broulee overlooks the beach, which is only a few hundred feet away. Inside, the house is beautifully and intelligently designed, with walls of glass facing the ocean and natural bush. Open windows and door, and the fresh clean air rushes through. Outside, there is a winding path from the house, through the bush, to the beach. Each walk along it is a little adventure. Looking south, the beach extends for more than a mile. Follow it around to the north, and you will be in the Broulee Island Nature Reserve. So no reason not to get plenty of beach walking in while staying there. Judy R. even took up running again, though only when it could be barefoot and along a beautiful beach. But most pleasant was to simply loll about on the beach in the late afternoon and watch the surfers bobbing on their boards in the deep blue distance.

There is a surfing school in Broulee and many of the students are so young you would be reluctant to let them cross the street by themselves. Yet there they are, gamely kicking, splashing and hauling their big boards over the near waves and out to the big ones. When at last one manages to kneel, then stand, and catch a ride, however brief, you can imagine the exultant grin even if you can't see it.

Often, as we walked along the beach, we saw people who were hunting for beach worms which they use as fishing bait. The hunt goes like this: take one leg from an old pair of pantyhose; stuff the toe end with the nastiest, smelliest fish heads you can find; around your waist, tie a bucket fashioned from an empty plastic milk jug; stand at the shallows dangling the yucky fish over the sand as the waves go out; watch for a worm to pop his head up; grab it and carefully work it up out of the sand before the waves come in again. This is no easy trick because the worms are a good ten inches long. We were glad to hear they don't come up for toes!

Also there was a glorious cacophony of exotic birds. Dawn and dusk bring a riot of chirps, peeps, squawks, and sometimes, the maniacal laughter of the kookaburra. We scattered parrot seed on one of the balconies and attracted a pair of crimson rosellas, who returned daily for their snack. One day when they did not finish it, we were visited at night by a ringtail possum—a creature who has little in common with his American cousin. As the name implies, instead of a skinny rat-like tail, the ringtail has a long, fancy, furry tail. Instead of tiptoeing timidly through the night, he launches himself from high places—trees branches, porch railings—with the gleeful abandon of a high-wire artist confident of a strong net, and then he lands with a resounding thump, perhaps to see how quickly you can sit bolt upright in bed and exclaim, "holy cow, what was that!?!" Once we were adjusted to his thumpings and bumpings in the night, we tried to sneak a photo, but the reflected glare of the flash on the window prevented us from getting a good one.

What with all the entertaining wildlife, it took us about a week of exploring the beaches in the area to get a good idea of all that the Eurobodalla Coast has to offer, which is a great deal. There are endless miles of beach broken by dramatic cliffs and rocky headlands. On a weekday, chances are good you will be the only person, or one of just a few, on any given beach. But it's not all a day at the beach. Also nearby are beautiful woodlands full of trees, bushes and ferns that are strange and exotic to the North American eye—eucalyptus, gum, and our favorite, the banksias. On one of our walks, where the woods were full of banksia trees, a sign at the trail head said, "This cliff top walk meanders through gnarled old man banksia . . . Old man banksias have captured the imagination of Australians for thousands of years. Aboriginal children are often instructed not to linger in these forests, as they are inhabited by mischievous spirits. May Gibbs in her classic tales of Snugglepot and Cuddlepie, turned old man banksia cones into 'Big Bad Banksia Men'."

Another day we drove to the Murramarang National Park, a coastal strip of scenic beaches and forests that includes Pebbly Beach, where close-and-personal wildlife is a given. No sooner did we alight from our car than colorful parrots swooped down to greet us, even alighting on shoulders and outstretched hands. In the nearby grassy area, gangs of kangaroos and wallabies casually grazed or boing, boing, boinged about just, so it seemed, for the fun of it. Park signs explicitly instructed not to feed the wildlife, but the gregariousness of the birds and roos and the presence of an atypically large number of human visitors suggested that the signs were often ignored. By contrast, on our trip to Monga National Park in the Great Dividing Range, we realized we were the only visitors. Though there were no kangaroos galumphing about, we loved the fresh eucalyptus-scented air and the cathedral-like quiet of the place broken only by the chirping of birds, the trickle of a stream, and the occasional rustling of a shy echinda in the underbrush.

Towns in the area ranged from Bateman's Bay, the largest and the gateway to the Eurobadalla Coast, to tiny Tilba, which is to the

An example of the wonderful geologic formations in the Broulee area.

south and one of Australia's only twenty officially designated Heritage Towns. Originally a gold mining town, Tilba today survives on tourists and local cheese, which is still made in the town. But for all Tilba's history, our favorite town was Moruya, which is there simply to serve its own folk.

Situated on a river of the same name, with a range of soft blue mountains in the background, Moruya is a small town with just about everything needed for a comfortable life—two grocery stores, two butchers, one bakery, two chemists (pharmacies), several restaurants, a news agent (newsstand), a video rental, a few auto or farm equipment dealers, a place to buy bait and fishing supplies, a Vinnie's (St. Vincent de Paul) shop by the Catholic church and a Salvo's (Salvation Army) store next to the Bi-Lo supermarket. Toss in a large heated community pool, a good fitness center, public tennis courts and golf course, the ubiquitous lawn bowls club, and a Saturday market, mix in the friendliest people you could ever meet, and what more could you want? Especially when you do something stupid like leave your purse in the Fish and Chips restaurant on the main street. That's what Judy did, and it wasn't until an hour and a half later, when we were ready to leave the gym, that we realized it was missing. Not finding it in the gym, we returned to the restaurant where we were greeted with the good news that we could stop worrying. They had taken the purse to the police station. At the police station where we retrieved it, they had carefully inventoried all the contents—credit cards, driver's license, (new) camera, little notebook of important jottings, a chapstick and an odd assortment of U.S., Fijian, Kiwi, and Australian currency. "No worries," said the policewoman who was working the desk, "it's all there, if a little mixed up since we had to do the inventory. You sure do get around, don't you?" "Yes," we thought later, and wished we'd said earlier, "and it's places like this town with people like you who make it such a wonderful, life-changing experience."

MONDAY, FEBRUARY 25, 2008

Farewell to Broulee and Canberra

One of the birds who greeted us at Pebbly Beach.

All too soon our time in Broulee came to an end, the final Friday spent in a series of last visits to the places and by the creatures that had become so familiar during our three wonderful weeks on the Eurobodalla Coast—a last drive along the lovely meandering river road that took us to Moruya, a last walk up over the dunes behind the house and onto the beach where swimmers and surfers bobbed in the deep blue sea between waves whose horizontal ribbons of white stretched to the horizon, and a last visit by the pair of crimson rosellas who by now knew that they would encounter no harm but find a welcoming scattering of seed on the porch. Then, the next day, it was pack up the car and drive back over the Great Dividing Range and on to Canberra.

Looming in Wayne's and Judy's driveway when we arrived at

their home was their latest acquisition, an eco-friendly "King of the Road" camper that can be towed over the roughest terrain, and which expands upwards and outwards to provide amazing creature comforts including a queen-size bed, satellite TV, a toilet, sink, and shower, and an outdoor kitchen that slides out with the flip of a latch. From the huge stack of manuals and instruction booklets that came with it, it was clear that a lot of reading would be required just to discover all the features and master their use.

Also spending the night with Wayne and Judy were the children of Judy's niece, Samantha, and her husband, Jason. Nick, 11, and Phoebe, 8, arrived around dinner and later, at the table, regaled us with tales of the family's summer spent traveling throughout the western U.S. and Canada. It was great fun to spend time with such bright, engaging kids who are so comfortable with themselves and others.

The next day, after Samantha and Jason had picked up Nick and Phoebe, we walked with Wayne and Judy into the hilly bush near their home. There, just as Wayne had promised, were scads of kangaroos. Though not overly shy, they were not fooled by our attempts to get closer by assuming kangaroo poses. So eventually, we walked back to the house, ate lunch and then, after hugs all around, it was off to the airport.

SATURDAY, MARCH 15, 2008

Arrival in Adelaide

Nagi, Judy, Eddy, Ann, Sam and Betty at Eddy's birthday dinner in Adelaide.

When we arrived in Adelaide, Nagi and Ann met us at the airport and took us to their second home—an apartment in Glenelg, Adelaide's closest and best-loved beach community. What has helped Glenelg become so popular is the tram that runs back and forth between Victoria Square in downtown Adelaide and Mosely Square in Glenelg, putting a day at the beach or night on the town within easy reach for anyone residing in Adelaide, Glenelg or the neighborhoods along the tram line. Yet despite being so close to the city, Glenelg is delightfully low key. Only one tall building, a round apartment complex, breaks the skyline. All else are small low-rise apartment buildings or, more often, lovingly maintained Federation-style bungalows and cottages dating to the early 1900s. Strolling the streets, passing baby buggys and other accoutrements of every-day life on front stoops, spying well-tended gardens only partially hidden by low walls of Adelaide twig fence, you are reassured that Glenelg is a place where people come not just to swim and sun, but to live.

Because we arrived in Glenelg on a Sunday afternoon, we only did a bit of unpacking and settling in before turning our attention to food—either finding a grocery store that was still open, or a restaurant. Across from the closest grocery, which in fact turned out to be closed, we spotted a Nepalese restaurant, Katmandu Palace, which thankfully was still open. It was so good that we made a mental note to return when our friends, Betty and Eddy Huang, arrived for a visit later in the week.

Before then, we decided to see as much of Adelaide as we could. Though Betty and Eddy would be with us almost a week, much of the time would be spent on a trip to Kangaroo Island, one of South Australia's "must see" attractions, leaving little time for the city. So hoping to be able to make the most of it, we took the tram from Glenelg and arrived at Victoria Square, which is at the center of this well-planned city. Laid out in a square grid and surrounded by parkland on all sides, Adelaide is hospitably designed and easy to negotiate. Though the capital of South Australia, it is on the smallish side, yet very urban in its vibe, its cultural offerings and its restaurants, for the folks in Adelaide are every bit as much foodies as the discriminating Melbournians.

You first sense this food vibe in the Central Market, which is open most days, and is a full city block crammed with purveyors of every imaginable edible, from fish to falafel, from chickens (or "chooks" as the Aussies call them) to hand-crafted organic cheeses, from sausages made in the rural town of Hahndorf to bakeries bursting with hot cross buns made especially for Easter. Nagi had told us that near closing time on Saturday, with the market not re-opening until Tuesday, the vendors "practically throw food at you" for super-low prices. Putting his claim to the test, we scored a perfect avocado, a mound of gorgeous red peppers, and a neat pile of perfect little Lebanese cucumbers, all for $4! The abundance in Adelaide's market is matched by the abundance and diversity of cuisines in its restaurants, many of

Betty feeding a joey (the last joey she fed like this was her daughter Joanna, nicknamed Joey).

which are located on the restaurant streets of Gouger, Hindley and Hutt.

We were delighted to be invited to dinner at one of Nagi and Ann's favorites, an Indian restaurant close to their city home and overlooking the park from East Terrace in downtown Adelaide. It was a very enjoyable and memorable occasion for us. But other leisurely meals would have to wait. We had more city to see before Betty and Eddy arrived, so in the next few days, we rushed pell mell from South Terrace to North, East Terrace to West, window shopped King William Street, the main north-south avenue and Rundle Mall, a pedestrian shopaholic's delight, and took time to wind down and cool off in the winding paths along the river Torrens that divides North Adelaide from Adelaide proper, and in the beautifully shady Botanical Garden. On one of those days, a Saturday, we saw several open-air weddings taking place. The custom seems to be: pick a nice park, rent some chairs, hire a caterer and a few limos, and voila, a lovely and not-too-pricey wedding. A bit hot, but no worries about rain.

Actually, more than a bit hot! Adelaide was then in the throes of a record heat wave, with temperatures 95 degrees or more most days. Though the record highs were at the top of the news every night, Adelaide natives seemed to take it in stride, having endured similar though shorter heat spells in the recent past. But it was wilting to visitors like us, hoping each day to cover more ground than turned out to be reasonable. They key, we learned was to do as the "siesta" cultures do—run errands in the morning, seek cool places in the heat of the day, and venture back out as the sun starts its descent and temperatures begin to drop.

In the midst of this long-running heat wave, Betty and Eddy arrived from Taipei to celebrate Eddy's 65th birthday and go with us to Kangaroo Island—perhaps the best place in Australia to easily see nearly all of the vast continent's iconic wildlife. So that first evening, Nagi and Ann came over for dinner to help join in honoring the birthday boy, and then the next morning we were off on our adventure.

TUESDAY, MARCH 18, 2008

Kangaroo Island

Two of the seals at Seal Bay on Kangaroo Island.

Though it is possible to fly to Kangaroo Island—there is a very small airport with a dirt runway—we chose, as do most, to take the Sealink ferry. Because we would only be on the island for three days, we found it would also be more economical to rent a car while there rather than taking ours on the boat. Having made those decisions, we than chose to avail ourselves of Sealink's door-to-shore coach service that would pick us up in Glenelg at 6:30 am and get us to Cape Jervis to take the 45-minute ferry ride across to Pennashaw on Kangaroo.

And what an efficient, fine-turned operation it turned out to be—bus on time down to the minute, reserved seats, ferry tickets distributed, luggage smoothly handled, and the very friendly Budget rental car fellow waiting for us when the ferry landed.

It was he who gave us a quick overview of Kangaroo Island and suggested we stop at the Tourist Information Center first thing. Which we did, and there encountered another very friendly, helpful person who essentially mapped out our plan to see and do as much as we possibly could in our three days. Considering the abundance of attractions, and the distances between them, we were already wondering if we could do justice to the island in such a short time. But thanks to all the helpful people we encountered, we feel we did—at least almost!

Our first stop was prosaic but necessary. On asking, we were told that the best-stocked grocery store on the island was in the town of Kingscote, about 50 miles away. So off we went, with a brief but very worthwhile stop to climb Prospect Hill, which stands on an isthmus and overlooks two beautiful bays. It was a good workout after our long boat ride, and gave us our first view of one of the island's many pristine beaches. Further along, lured by a dot on the map labeled "American River," we detoured to find, beside a broad river—home to pelicans, ibises, and many other waterbirds—a small village that while sleepy and rather non-descript today, was once the favored landfall for American whalers.

By contrast, Kingscote, the site of the first settlement in South Australia, is quite lively. In addition to being home to about half of Kangaroo Island's 3000 permanent residents and the service town for nearly all of them, it's the one place tourists can find the essentials they'll need for their visit. One can, of course, also find the usual T-shirts, key fobs and other souvenirs there, too. But most tourists soon realize, as we did, that the most cherished souvenirs of Kangaroo Island are pictures and memories.

Though the heat had been oppressive in Adelaide, it was worse on the island. We had been forewarned that temperatures had reached into the 90s every day, and to 100 more often than not. By the time we arrived at Kangastay, the little house we had rented for our stay at Vivonne Bay, located on the middle south coast of the island, we were wilting fast. We unpacked our groceries, opened the windows to catch a bit of breeze, then collapsed until hunger spurred us to get up, go for a short explore, and later fix dinner.

Things to expect in your Kangaroo Island rental house: simple furnishings, comfortable beds, sheets and towels, a well-equipped kitchen with a modicum of staples, an assortment of puzzles and games, several water tanks and only one bathroom with, to boot, a timer on the shower. Peruse the rental options and you will find few rentals that offer luxurious furnishings—it's an island, after all, and everything must be shipped by sea—and even fewer that have additional baths, regardless of the number of bedrooms. Because Kangaroo Island has no underground source of fresh water, there is a perpetual severe water shortage, just how severe depending on the amount of rainfall during the wetter winter months. Short-term visitors could ignore the shower timers and soak and splash to their hearts' content, but thankfully few do.

By the next morning, we were sufficiently revived to better tolerate the heat, and so we set off to see more of the island, stopping first in the center in the little town of Pardana. Judy was the one with a special interest in seeing Pardana and its surroundings, primarily because of sheep. To put it plainly, she has an odd and inexplicable fondness for sheep. In traveling the dusty, unpaved roads of the island's interior, much to her delight, there were sheep over every hill and around every corner. But in Pardana proper, there were things to delight us all.

Pardana is in the middle of the vast dry center of Kangaroo Island. Drive through it, and you will quickly pass the bottle shop, the IGA grocery, the feed and hardware store, and be back on the dusty, dirt road that for a short section serves as its main street. But stop, walk around a bit, visit the community center which also houses a museum, talk to a few residents, and you find a town rich in history and friendly people happy to share their stories.

The first story we heard was that of Mrs. Wetherall, a lovely woman of 90 years who, when we entered, was the only person in the shop run by the local spinning and weaving guild. The organization's simple brochure explains that the guild was started by an Adelaide woman who had ties to the community, and though Pardana is tiny, the guild has a membership of over 40 women. It was from Mrs. Wetherall herself that we learned that these particular spinners and weavers are involved in their craft from sheep to shop. Most of them help raise the sheep, participate in their shearing, and gather from the bush and shore the natural materials they use to hand dye the wool they spin and then weave or knit into hats, scarves, sweaters, and fanciful little baby toys. "When I was younger," she said as she sat at her spinning wheel, "my husband and I would go to the beach, where I would scrape this special lichen from the rocks. It made the most heavenly shade of mauve. Oh, it made the most beautiful yarn. I can't do that anymore, or even knit or weave, because of my arthritis. But I'm so glad I can still do this," she smiled, as her feet danced lightly on the pedals and the wool slipped smoothly through her fingers. We all left there feeling blessed. Judy left with a new hat as well. It's not something she'd wear in the Australian heat wave, but it would provide warmth and warm memories the next winter in Washington.

Curious to learn more about Pardana, we decided to drop into the community center and visit the Pardana Soldier Settlement Museum, which documents the saga of the returning World War II soldiers, many with wives and children, who had struggled to claim new land and lives on the island. In a simple room, no larger than your average coffee shop, where the underside of the corrugated roof shows gray and rusting through the rafters, are the maps, manuals, and scale models produced by the government that sought to recruit the settlers, along with the diaries, scrapbooks, and iconic necessities—dishpans and plows, saws and sewing machines, cricket bats and chamberpots—brought by those who came. In less than a decade, these few hundred families transformed Kangaroo Island, clearing bush and forest to create farms, sheep stations, and the village of Pardana. Though most failed as farmers, some of the original settlers made a go of it, eventually adding to their holdings as others gave up and sold out. Today, the children and grandchildren of those who stayed witness with ambivalence a second transformation that is taking place on the western end of Kangaroo Island, close by Flinders Chase National Park. This is where timber companies are buying whatever land they can on which to plant blue gum trees, which grow rapidly and are good for pulp. Driving through, you see row upon row of these blue gums, steadily marching to the horizon and returning the land if not to its original state, to one in greater harmony with its more distant past.

From Pardana, where we had spent more time than we had expected, we hurried on to Paul's Place, where we still hoped to keep to our plan to take part in the noon tour. Paul's Place defies simple description. Call it a wildlife park, or worse, a roadside zoo, and you would likely cringe and wonder what it is doing on Kangaroo Island. Call it a working farm that has some resident wildlife and some chores you can help with, and you would likely want to visit. Arriving at Paul's Place with open minds and in the nick of time, we joined several dozen other people, including families with kids, and were given the run with a friendly gaggle of kangaroos, wallabies, emus, koalas, cockatoos and kookaburras, and one big snake, all of whom mingled happily with the more prosaic sheep and lambs, chickens and ducks, and oddly, one deer. Though all the feeding, nuzzling, and picture taking took place in enclosures, it was only a few little humans who seemed to want to get away. Paul is very respectful of the animals, and interacting with them is a happy, rollicking experience for both adults and children. But there were a few toddlers who were set to wailing by the sheer size of the emus and larger kangaroos.

However, all the kids loved riding the ponies, exploring the shearing shed and watching Paul shear a sheep. In the shed—a large barn with many stalls and levels to explore—young and old paid rapt attention as one hapless ewe, manipulated and held in a variety of contorted and undignified positions, got the mother of all haircuts. Once separated from her fleece, she was released to the outdoors, while the children were boosted up onto the sorting wheel and spun around as the air resounded with their shrieks and giggles. As the wheel slowed, Paul scooped them up one by one and carefully but energetically tossed them into a huge pile of fleece. With all that excitement, plus a ride on their choice of the fast pony or the slow one, it would be no surprise to learn that all the children envied Paul's daughter and constant shadow, four-year-old Poppy, who gets to do stuff like that every day.

Leaving Paul's Place, we continued north to Stokes Bay, where you must carefully thread your way between walls of rocks to get to the beach. It's an adventure in its own right, and well worth it. The beach is beautiful, with a large horseshoe bend where the waves delight surfers and boogie boarders, and a protected area of clear water, no deeper than chest high, where moms can relax while children splash and play, and reef fish can be spotted even without snorkel gear. As idyllic as it was, just a handful of other people were there, and at the next breathtaking beach, Snelling, we saw only a lone woman frolicking with her dog. Viewed from the high road above, they were just two dark dots on a beautiful vista of sea, sand, and sky. Reluctantly, we headed back to Vivonne Bay, stopping at a place known as Koala Walk and easily spotting nearly a dozen snoozing koalas in less than half an hour.

On our last day, we went to see the big three Kangaroo Island attractions, the must-sees even for those who only come for a day trip: Seal Bay, Remarkable Rocks, and Admirals Arch. Seal Bay is a protected area for sea lions. Though none too graceful on land, they could easily waddle around rocky outcrops up or down the beach to more private spots where humans aren't allowed. But they seemed to prefer the more exposed area despite our presence. Credit goes to the parks department and its staff who designed the series of non-intrusive boardwalks, some to overlooks from which can be seen the entire vista of the beach and dramatic cliffs, and to the engaging but no-nonsense ranger/guides who lead small, tightly controlled groups onto the beach to observe the seals from a discreet distance. Of the dozens of seals on the beach, most were lumbering or dozing males, largely ignoring their baby-sitting duties, while the little ones whined and wailed. When our guide was asked why the little ones seemed so distressed, she explained that they were waiting for their mothers who, in order to insure adequate nourishment to sustain lactation, had to leave them and hunt and feed for days at a time. She also responded with what all of the women in our group agreed was remarkable restraint when one asked, "Well, can't the husbands go catch fish?"

Our next stop was Remarkable Rocks, where to a large extent your degree of appreciation depends on your level of agility. The more you clamor and climb upon the rock formations, the more varied and amazing the views, with the uppermost ones offering wonderful panoramas of the unspoiled seashore. Finally, we went to Admiral's Arch, a hidden wonder that you only see after walking down several winding flights of stairs to where, at the bottom, you discover the high natural rock arch that opens onto rock pools of frolicking seals, and then to the crashing sea.

To say that Kangaroo Island exceeded our every expectation is probably stating the obvious. But it did, and we think it deserves a place on anyone's wish list of places to visit.

WEDNESDAY, MARCH 26, 2008

Back in Adelaide

Bronze pigs on Rundle Street in Adelaide doing what pigs do.

After we returned from Kangaroo Island, Betty and Eddy still had a day to see more of Adelaide. As the historic heat wave continued, we took the tram in to town, got off at Victoria Square, and walked over to the Central Market. It being a Saturday, with the market not open again until Tuesday, it was especially lively and, as closing time approached, thronged with bargain hunters hoping to get some last minute deals. We synchronized our watches to go our separate ways and meet up back by the sausage stand just outside the main hall in 45 minutes. During that time, Betty and Eddy found a $5 leather belt for Eddy, and Judy and Sam snagged a huge bag of yummy, just-roasted nuts.

All that hunting and gathering had made us hungry, so we then went into Chinatown, where we decided to have a late lunch in a large bustling food court—a virtual crossroads of Asian cuisines and people. Once again, after finding a table, we each went our own way to choose and order what we wanted, and all returned with something everyone wanted to taste. Betty even came back with a story of meeting a fellow Taiwanese woman who had come to Adelaide some years ago, started her business there in the food court, and had much to say about what a wonderful place Adelaide was to live and raise a family. After lunch, we visited the statuesque pigs of the Rundle Street pedestrian mall, found a few bargains, sought a bit of shade in the nearby and lovely Botanical Gardens, and finished the day with a visit to the Migration Museum, which chronicles the country's decades of ambivalence regarding the need for immigrants.

The next day, after taking Betty and Eddy to the airport for their return to Taipei—they would also stop over to spend a few days with friends in Hong Kong—we stayed close to "home," enjoying Glenelg. The following day Kerry and Richard, our friends from Melbourne, arrived, bringing with them a very welcome gift. When we left their home in Melbourne they had given us a small jar of tomato relish to take with us. Kerry, we were told, had made it from a family recipe, and at the time, we thought, "Well, how nice," and set it aside. It was only later when we opened the jar and tasted the contents that we realized we had been given a delectable treasure, and immediately sent off a shamelessly groveling email for the recipe. Thanks be to friends who arrive not only with the recipe, but another nice big jar of tomato relish! Kerry had also brought with her a lot of information on shopping and restaurants given her by a friend who had lived in Adelaide. So the next day, off we went to shop and lunch in Unley and Hyde Park, two close-in attractive neighborhoods in Adelaide's prosperous eastern fringes. That evening, we went to one of the recommended restaurants, Good Time Organic Pizza, which has locations in both Glenelg and the city. We all agreed their reputation for having the best pizza in Adelaide was well-deserved.

The following day, as the record heat wave continued, the four of us decided to visit the Adelaide Zoo, which is a lovely old 19th century creation with many features of more modern zoos. Our primary mission: to see a wombat. It's true that most zoo goers are apt to make a beeline for the lions, tigers and elephants—not these rotund, furry creatures that are unique to Australia. But having fallen in love with a darling children's book, Wombat Goes Walkabout, and located copies for all our grandchildren, we wanted to see the protagonist of the charming story in the fur, so to speak. But sadly, all we did was hear him. The day being so hot, he was in the shady corner of his little yard batting a metal bucket around and making a ruckus in protest, we assume, for the fact that the door to his cooler little cave-like dwelling was blocked. So we satisfied ourselves with seeing the more exotic animals, including Australia's ridiculously large number of snakes that have enough poison to kill just about anything ten times over, and taking a coffee break in the landscaped gardens by the zoo's big, beautiful ironwork gazebo.

That evening, Ann and Nagi were able to come to dinner again, bringing with them wine and a wonderful pate. Then, early the next morning, Richard and Kerry were up and out to begin their long drive back to Melbourne in the cool of the morning.

It was almost time for us to leave Adelaide, too, and with so much to see and do, we were torn about how to spend our last several days. In the end, we decided to spend one day in Victor Harbor, where we took a scenic circular walk around Granite Island; visit McLaren Vale and the Barossa Valley, South Australia's most famous wine regions; and on our last day, do a farewell walkabout of Adelaide, which after three wonderful weeks, felt very much like home.

Judy standing beside a Moreton Bay fig tree.

MONDAY, APRIL 7, 2008

Noosa - Part I

"He was not bone and feather but a perfect idea of freedom and flight, limited by nothing at all."

— *Richard Bach, Jonathan Livingston Seagull*

Our Noosa Heads exchange partners, Chris Murray and Lizzie Cook, had left us their car at the airport parking lot in Brisbane with directions and a map to their house. That and the good roads going up to Noosa made it easy for us to get to their house—a light-filled, open-plan house with a pool in a small gated community in the heart of Noosa Heads.

Coming back to Noosa after five years felt a little like coming home. For the most part, we knew which roads to take to get around and what we would find if we went another way. Some of

After you climb the steep slope of Mount Coorora you are rewarded with a view from the top.

the first things we wanted to see were the things we remembered, and for which Noosa is famous: the beach at Laguna Bay, the national park with its miles of walking trails and magnificent views, the shops and cafes along Hastings Street, and Gympie Terrace, which weaves its way along the Noosa River, lush parkland on one side and casual restaurants and shops on the other. On our earlier visit, we had been spellbound the first time we witnessed the squadrons of brilliantly colored rainbow lorikeets that at dusk came swooping and squawking from all directions to alight in the trees along the river. Five years later, the free show and our gratitude for it were the same.

We were also eager to re-visit the Eumundi market, which is held on Wednesdays and Saturdays, and the Noosa Farmers' Market. Both had prospered in the five years we were away and now were bigger and better than ever. The Noosa market especially had become a cornucopia of fresh organic meats and produce, artisan breads and cheeses, locally made wine, and a world tour of relishes, curry pastes, and all manner of items to take home as well as crepes, German sausages and other goodies to eat on the spot.

As we parked and entered the Noosa market, we heard the sounds of an acoustic guitar and a wonderful rugged baritone voice that sounded for all the world like John Prine with an Aussie accent. It turned out to be a Jimmy Howard, an older man from the Northern Territories and the Alice Springs area, doing a song made famous by Slim Dusty, an icon of Australian country music. We were so taken with the voice and the song, a mournful version of "Waltzing Matilda" decrying environmental and social degradation, that we asked Jimmy if he would mind if we videotaped him singing it again, which he graciously did. Listening to it again back in our exchange home, and watching the video, we felt we had come upon a real treasure. In thanks, we bought a copy of all the CDs Jimmy Howard had to sell, and made a DVD of Jimmy singing the song that had so captured our attention. We gave him his copy a week later at the Noosa Market, and made two others—one for us and one for Chris and Lizzie.

Noosa National Park must be one of the world's most accessible national parks. One minute you're on the beach or window shopping on Hastings Street, and the next you're on the elevated boardwalk as it ascends through the trees along the coast and into the park. The only decision at that point is whether to focus on the beautiful vistas or watch for koalas in the trees along the way. But upon reaching the park with its bird's eye view back to the beach, there is the decision of which trail to take. Choices include one along the coastline past hidden and nearly deserted beaches, or the inland rambles that take you along dry sandy trails of banksia and then drop you into lush green rainforest. No matter, all are spectacular, and more likely than not you'll spot bush turkeys, goannas and koalas along the way.

Not far from the park, where the Noosa River enters the sea, is an area called Noosaville. Along Gympie Terrace, the road that follows the river and on one side is lined with shops and restaurants, runs the verdant riverside park where the swarms of rainbow lorikeets put on their nightly show. There you can have a cookout, rent a kayak or pontoon boat, ride a ferry that shuttles passengers from Noosa, along the river, and to the marina farther upstream in Tewantin, or fish from the shore or public pier. One Sunday afternoon, as dusk approached, we spent several hours on the pier with two young brothers who delighted in out fishing us. There we were with our pricey bait and fancy traveler's telescoping rod and reel; there they were with their simple handlines and a bit of leftover shrimp they had begged from their mum, and they easily caught three fish for our every one. The most spectacular catch, again by one of the youngsters, was a good-size stingray that caused quite a commotion before it was released, with great care we might add, by a father who clearly did not want to go the way of Steve Irwin.

There's a bit of ambivalence here, as elsewhere, about Steve Irwin, the famous, and now deceased, star of Crocodile Hunter and founder of the Australia Zoo. Having passed the zoo traveling

Fraser Island, a day trip from Noosa, is the world's largest sand island and a World Heritage Site.

to and from Noosa back in 2003, we decided this time to stop for a visit. Overall, we came away feeling that it was well-managed but grossly commercial, with every special "experience," such as a petting photo-op with a koala, separately and exorbitantly priced. A reverential biography of Irwin, written by his widow and presumably seeking wide readership, was priced at $39.95.

When our search for a local gym yielded the one at Noosa Springs resort, we felt like we were in the offshore tax haven league. Having some time ago reached that time of life in which exercise is not just a good thing, but an absolute necessity in order to fend off excess pounds and try to maintain our health, we are always interested in finding a good gym when we travel. One of the best in our experience was Mauna Lani resort on the Big Island of Hawaii, which has a modern fitness facility and a wonderful pool connected to it, all available for a reasonable day rate. So here in Noosa, we looked for a similar situation and were delighted to find Noosa Springs. It's quite a posh resort, with gated neighborhoods, a golf course and all the accoutrements of resort living. But happily, the fitness center and lap pool are available to the public at a reasonable day rate, and as it was with Mauna Lani, they are not heavily used, probably because people visiting a resort are not really going there to swim laps and sweat on cross trainers. In any case, we reveled in having both the gym and pool almost to ourselves on most days.

On one special day, we almost had a mountain to ourselves. It was only by accident that we wound up climbing Mount Coorora. We had set out in mid-morning to hike a trail along Lake Cootharaba. But at the Point Elanda trailhead, the trail went into woods that looked wet and buggy, so we drove what we thought was north to find another entrance to the trail. After several turns on unsigned, rural roads, the lake was nowhere in sight and we realized we were headed not north but west toward the small hinterland town of Pomona. Needing a plan B, we consulted our book of hikes in the area and saw there was a hike up nearby Mt.

If you are lucky, you may be greeted by Captain Cook himself (who is now well over 200 years old).

Coorora which was described as "very difficult." Now back home, where "moderate" often means "must be able to remain upright" and "very difficult" could mean "slight elevation, uneven path," we would have ignored the warning. But here in Oz, where next up from "very difficult" is "Crikey, you gotta be crazy," we took it to heart and decided to just go up as far as the first lookout.

When we got there, we were a bit winded, but also disappointed in the view. "So," we said to one another, "why not go a little higher, just to see what it's like," and again, off we went up through a bit of woods, around a bend, and there in front of us was a rock pile that went straight up, forever so it sometimes seemed. In some places, steps were carved into the rocks; in others, attached to iron poles was a heavy chain that you could use to haul yourself upwards; and in some places there was nothing except the tantalizing feeling that a million dollar view was "just a little further up." Which is how we enticed ourselves all the way to the top of Mount Coorora.

And the view was fantastic: 360 views back to Noosa and out to sea; the vast hinterlands rolling out to the west; and other mountains rising alone and abruptly from the land in all directions. We drank our water, basked on warm rocks, explored the ridge that was cooled by a fresh breeze, and procrastinated as long as we could before starting what we knew would be a tough climb back down the mountain.

It had taken us about two hours to haul ourselves up the mountain; whereas coming down was mostly a matter of resisting the pull of gravity; ignoring the complaints of tired muscles, and in more than a few places, easing along on our backsides. Going up and coming down, we were passed by several younger, fitter and faster hiker-climbers, but we think it's a fair guess to say that none felt as proud of themselves or enjoyed the adventure as much as we did! So . . . good on us!

FRIDAY, APRIL 11, 2008

Noosa - Part II

Judy charming the (plastic) crocodile at Australia Zoo.

When we visited Noosa five years earlier, our explorations had hugged the coastline, so we were not aware of the beauty of the hinterlands around Noosa. In the information they'd left for us, Chris and Lizzie had suggested a drive along the wine and art trail that winds through the foothills and into the Blackall Range, which also affords views of the fancifully shaped

Glasshouse Mountains to the south. We took their advice one beautiful day and found not only scenery that was different from, but every bit as breathtaking as that along the coast, but also afforded many nice walking trails. A favorite was Fig Tree Walk, a short loop that winds through the rainforest past ancient Moreton Bay fig trees.

We also explored the coastal area south of Noosa almost as far as Caloundra, and found below Maroochydore many beach communities with beautiful walks along the shore. One featured a touching monument in tribute to the "soldier" dogs that served Australia in the two world wars and in Vietnam. Many community parks included outdoor exercise equipment—simple sturdy versions of typical gym equipment, but painted in bright colors and designed to be used outdoors. The signs indicating "for adults only" made the equipment irresistible to children, which we suspect was part of a creative plot to help Australia avoid the level of obesity for which the U.S. is known worldwide.

We had both put on an extra kilo or two ourselves, due in part to the fabulous kitchen that had awaited us when we arrived at our Noosa exchange home. Though we thought we had pretty good knives back home in our own kitchens, we found ourselves lusting after a new set of Globals. Also impressive were the gleaming gas stove with a burner especially intended for wok cooking and a gorgeous, non-stick wok with a stand to keep it just the right height above the fire. Together, these inspired us to try a few recipes from Lizzie's stash of "Delicious" magazines—published by the Australian public broadcasting system, and without a doubt the world's best food mag—and to take one more stab at making Singapore rice noodles, one of our favorite dishes. We had tried to make it a few years earlier without great success, but this time, following a new recipe, it turned out better than we could have hoped. We patted ourselves on the back and agreed with each other that our Singapore rice noodles were as good as you could get. Whether we could obtain the same result in a lesser kitchen was a challenge we expected to take up when we got back home.

During this trip we had received a home exchange inquiry from Noosa residents Karen and John Berghauser, and though we had to tell them that we were already booked for a Noosa exchange, we suggested that we would nevertheless enjoy meeting up with them. So one Sunday morning, we met for coffee at the nearby Tewantin Marina, site of a weekly market. Later in the week, they invited us to dinner at their home. Also there was an Australian-American couple (he had lived in suburban Maryland), and we had a great time discussing America and Australia, home exchanging, retirement and other subjects. Karen and John were then still working, she as a teacher and he as the administrator of a private Lutheran school, but because Australian educators receive a sabbatical of many months after each ten years of service, they hoped to soon embark on an ambitious around-the-world adventure. Knowing that they hoped to include several days in DC, and realizing that our apartment would be available for the dates they had planned, we offered it to them. In truth, we weren't sure we would ever return to Noosa, but we knew we would appreciate an opportunity to "pay forward" our gratitude for all the hospitality and many kindnesses we've enjoyed over the years from the home exchange community.

On our last day in Noosa, we had much to do to get our lovely exchange house in good order and get ready to depart the next day for Sydney. Still, we couldn't resist one last trip to the lovely Noosa Springs gym and pool we had so enjoyed during our stay and where, once again, we had the place almost to ourselves. It was the sort of day we wished we could put in a bottle and take back out when needed. But instead, we resolved to do our best to remember it as a perfect day in a perfect place in a perfect part of the world.

WEDNESDAY, APRIL 30, 2008

Sydney

Bryan, Trina, Sam & Judy in a photo from our first trip to Australia.

Two of the things we were most looking forward to on our return to Sydney were reconnecting with Bryan and Trina Hodgson, friends we met on our earlier trip, and finally meeting former exchange partners, Bee and John Cogger. We had stayed in Bee and John's bright, spacious apartment in Mosman in 2003, while they simultaneously had stayed in our DC apartment and visited Hidden Valley, our country place in Virginia. But as so often happens in our home exchanges, the only people who had met Bee and John were some of our neighbors on California Street and Randall, our dear friend, now deceased, who had taken care of Hidden Valley for us. We felt we knew Bee and John well through Bee's entertaining, newsy emails over the years, so it was with great sadness that we learned John had died very recently, and that Bee was soldiering on and getting ready to move alone to a new home and new life in Queensland that she and John had hoped to share. We were very grateful that despite all the turmoil in her life, Bee was able to meet us for coffee one morning, and not at all surprised to be as charmed by Bee in person as we had been by Bee in cyberspace.

Bryan and Trina Hodgson were the first people we met in Sydney on our trip five years earlier, and again, it was a friendship that had begun through emails. We had been in touch with them to see if they would be interested in a simultaneous home exchange, and though they could not do one at the time, they very kindly offered to let us stay with them if we did not find an exchange. In the end, we arranged an exchange with Bee and John, but we continued to stay in touch with Bryan and Trina, and it was he who met us at the airport back in 2003 and hauled us and our ridiculous amount of luggage all the way to our exchange home (Bee and John's) in Mosman. On meeting up with Bryan and Trina this time, we were happy to report that we had learned to travel at least nominally lighter, and it was a joy to catch up and gad about with these dear, generous friends again.

Mosman is one of several upmarket suburbs on the northern shore of Sydney harbor, and from our apartment it was about a twenty minute walk downhill to catch a ferry bound for Circular Quay. But there was another option that we especially loved: walking a footpath that winds along the foreshore to Cremorne Point and all the way to Neutral Bay. The walk is a visual feast of coves dotted with moored sailboats, beautiful homes and gardens, and one special garden lovingly created out of what had been a dumping ground by two people, Lex and Ruby Graham, whose courtship and long and happy marriage was nurtured by the love of gardening and their desire to create a beautiful space for everyone to enjoy. Their protective spirit lives on in the attitudes and actions of most who live along the walkway. At a point along the walkway where stood a dead but still standing tree near a looming house with a curiously rare, unobstructed view of the water, the local council had placed a billboard-size sign that read, "Warning—this tree has been willfully destroyed by selfish vandals. $10,000 reward offered for information leading to a successful prosecution. Penalty for breaching North Sydney Council Tree Preservation Order up to $1.1 million." The sign also helpfully provided a contact number to receive the information. We can only guess at who they thought the vandals might be!

During the period we were in Sydney, we revisited most of the usual tourist sights—Circular Quay, the Opera House, the Rocks, the Botanical Garden, the stores at the Queen Victoria Building, some of the museums, Watson's Bay, and Paddington. Not to be missed, not even on an umpteenth trip to Sydney, is the wonderful Taronga Zoo, where the animals, especially the giraffes, have a million-dollar view of Sydney.

One of the places that Judy especially wanted to see was the home of May Gibbs. Gibbs lived and worked in Sydney for many years in a Neutral Bay house that is now open to visitors. In a nod to the creator of Peter Rabbit and other loveable animal characters so familiar to British and American children, Gibbs is considered Australia's Beatrix Potter. In her charming stories and illustrations, Gibbs similarly used the iconic animals and plants of Australia to instill in Aussie children a special love for their country's unique culture. In recognition of her creativity and accuracy, Gibbs is today considered one of the early naturalists of Australia, and we would heartily recommend a visit to her home for anyone hoping to gain an appreciation of Aussie character and culture.

Although the weather had been rainy for much of our stay in Sydney, with our departure date not far off and time running out, we decided to go by train to the Blue Mountains, a place we had missed seeing on our first trip to Australia. The weather was still iffy on our day of departure, but we hoped that by staying in the area two days we would be able to finally see the fantastical Three Sisters rock formations and other sights. But no! There was rain and fog the entire time we were there, and at the local office where tours are arranged, we learned these conditions had persisted for eleven days. The twinkly-eyed counter attendant said, "It's been so long since we've seen them, even we aren't sure the Three Sisters are still there!" and we departed the next day being no more sure than he.

Ah well, to dedicated travelers and home exchangers, in such disappointments lie the hopes and justifications for return visits.

Request for Review

Over the past twenty years we have introduced many people to home exchange and have shared our home exchange stories and experiences with many more. Some of our friends have told us we really ought to provide the information we have accumulated in a book. This is that book.

If you enjoyed it and think it would be useful to those who may be considering home exchange, we would be very grateful for your positive review. Rest assured, we read all reviews and appreciate all comments and suggestions. You can post your review on the Amazon web page for our book.

We invite you to also visit our blog, where we further discuss home exchange and related topics and where you can find such materials as a free, comprehensive guide to getting your home ready for a home exchange.

You can visit our blog at www.goldenyearstravel.com.

About the Authors

S am and Judy Robbins live in Washington, DC. Having been "golden years" travelers since their retirements, they have done over 70 home exchanges.

For years they have been talking about home exchanging with friends, family and people they meet along the way and explaining the many benefits of home exchange.

This year their enthusiasm for home exchange finally boiled over and they wrote this book and developed a website devoted to inexpensive travel, with home exchange as the key strategy.

32334860R00085

Made in the USA
Middletown, DE
31 May 2016